Waterfowling Boats, Blinds & Related Gear

"Your duck boat comes next in line behind your trusted retriever. Treat it well and you will have two friends the next time you head out to your favorite hunting location. Neglect it and some day it may 'let you down'.

Chuck Lichon

Duck Hunters
October 1939, Chippewa County , Michigan

Contents

Printed by Rogers Printing Incorporated, Ravenna, MI

Cover photo by Chuck Lichon, on the Saginaw Bay, Michigan November 1996

Printed in the U.S.A.

Library of Congress Cataloging in Publication Data
97-094138

Lichon, Chuck
Waterfowling Boats, Blinds & Related Gear

Introduction

My early introduction to hunting came when I was around age nine or ten. I always took the opportunity to tag along with anyone who would let me join them, whether it be in pursuit of the wily pheasant or bounding whitetail. The world of waterfowling, however, was largely unknown to me at this early age.

One day Bill, who is one of three older brothers of mine asked me to go along on a duck hunt with a hunting companion of his by the name of Tom Haley. Tom was born into a family of avid hunters; something you would quickly guess when you walked into their house. Even in June you would find a 12-gauge side-by-side leaning up against the living room wall, or a pair of old canvas waders lying near the utility room from the previous season. The house looked more like a hunting lodge during the latter part of the waterfowl season than a typical American home.

We headed out to the east side of the historic Saginaw Bay, a sportsman paradise unparalleled by none in those days. It may have been near Fish Point, about halfway up the area known as Michigan's Thumb, but I cannot recall for sure. I remember getting out of the car on a cold, windy, cloudy day. Fluttering wings of ducks could be seen everywhere, seemingly as if they knew a noreasterly was about to soon push them further south. A permanent blind was situated only a few hundred feet off shore in shallow water, but still too deep for my knee-high boots. My brother offered to carry me on his back to the blind, but the better half of my brain told me this may not be such a good idea. Blue jeans and cold water mix about as well as milk and gin.

My brother and his friend slowly worked their way out to the blind while I watched from shore. I can still picture myself sitting next to a small tree, watching the ducks rock back and forth in the wind, as if they were in a panic. A snapshot of days gone by.

It was not until high school in the mid 1960s that I finally took on waterfowling. As is the case with most beginner waterfowlers, I did not have all the gear or money to buy it. Delivering newspapers, playing football, and other activities prevented me from actively pursuing waterfowl. Ironically, one of Tom's younger brothers, Fred, who was a year younger than me, invited me on a duck hunt at the Shiawassee State Game Area, also known as the "Flats". The Flats consist of an area of 10,000 prime wetland acres near my hometown of Saginaw, Michigan. With gun in hand, and the Haley collection of decoys, boat, motor and other gear, this was my first real opportunity to duck hunt.

Several more years went on before I managed to acquire more than a pair of leaky waders to hunt waterfowl. College managed to interfere with my main interests, but eventually things fell into place. A second job and several thousand dollars later I had enough equipment to be self-sufficient. I never forgot these early experiences, and if nothing else it made me realize that numerous kids are in the same boat, so to speak. No money, no gear, no tutor, no hunting.

Waterfowling is not the easiest and certainly not the least expensive of the hunting sports. Boat, motor, trailer, blind material, waders, gun, decoys, not to mention your retriever who spends more time at the vet than in the marsh, along with a four wheel vehicle to pull all this gear, places us in a class of financial misfits.

Waterfowlers would rather buy a new pair of neoprene waders than rent a tux for the son's wedding. When your better half gets in the family vehicle she needs to wear protective outerwear to prevent all the mud and water from ruining her clothes. And what once was a two-car garage, now turns into a storage facility for all this gear during the waterfowl season. Discarded pieces of conduit are sculptured into a boat or field blind once it gets in the hands of a waterfowler. Old barrels are used as the base for a floating blind large enough to accommodate four hunters and a dog. Don't talk recycling to a duck hunter; we have been doing it for decades.

Waterfowlers are not generally considered to be cheap by any stretch of the imagination. Even though we look for inexpensive waterfowl gear, we don't hesitate to buy what we need when the opportunity presents itself. Waterfowlers are always seeking methods to improve on what we may already own, the love of waterfowling precludes any notion of being a miser when it comes to our equipment. Many of us may tend to look for bargains, or try to make do with a discarded piece of equipment.

Hence the writing of this book. It is intended to be a useful, practical guide to boats, blinds and related

Hence the writing of this book. It is intended to be a useful, practical guide to boats, blinds and related gear. With it I hope you generate some ideas of your own, methods to make your time spent in the marsh easier, safer, and overall more successful; success measured in terms of enjoying the out-of-doors and what it has to offer, meeting friends with mutual interests, and not total number of birds in the bag. Refer to this book often, think about improving on what you already have. Although I have not personally tried all the ideas outlined in this book, and certainly cannot comment on their seaworthiness, I trust you will use good judgement in the design and use of your boat or blind. If the ore carrying freighter Edmund Fitzgerald could have a tragic day on Lake Superior, so can you. Always keep in mind that no matter what you build or how well you may think you build something, nothing can compete with the forces of nature. Even seasoned, intelligent veterans have managed to loose the battle with Mother Nature.

With that in mind, I hope you enjoy this book, and will someday create a waterfowl craft that is passed down to generations of kids and grandkids.

Chuck Lichon

Jill

"To All Our Retrievers: Past, Present, and Future"

Acknowledgments

I would like to thank the waterfowl fraternity who graciously assisted in the content of this book by allowing me to use many of their designs and ideas. Thanks to many others who also assisted including close friends and hunting buddies for allowing me to expose them in this book to the world of waterfowlers; to Nancy Clay who threw me a computer (program) lifesaver, assisting me greatly in the technical production of this book; to my kids Michelle and Jeff who allowed me to use my computer even when they had important college papers to complete; to all those special individuals, some being non-hunters, who spent time assisting during several of my photo shoots; to the commercial operations listed on the covers as well as in the commercial section of this book, who willingly helped with part of the significant financial support required to produce this book; and to you, the reader, who obviously has an interest in an outdoor activity second to none.

A very special note of thanks goes out to Michigan wildlife artist and friend, Jim Campbell, who provided the art sketches for the chapter headings.

~1~ Field Blinds

Hunting ducks or geese in a crop field is popular with waterfowlers for several reasons: 1) No need for lugging your boat or motor, 2) No need for waders, 3) Spared from setting out dozens of decoys in water conditions that would send chills up the back of a freighter captain, 4) Access to hunting site is generally much easier, and 5) Birds, when working a field, often are in larger flocks, providing plenty of action.

A drawback to field hunting is that a field may be "hot" one day, and totally dead the next. "Burn out" is a certainty if hunters overuse a field. Although this condition is also true in marsh areas, it seems to be more prevalent in dry crop fields.

For a beginner hunter, field hunting can be relatively inexpensive and is an easy way to be introduced to waterfowl hunting. A blind can consist of simply lying on a piece of impermeable material and covering up with camo, either the natural material found in the field, or an artificial covering like burlap. Although dozens of field decoys are required, the rag decoys or silhouettes work well, and are relatively inexpensive.

Other simple field blind possibilities include a wood or metal framework covered with natural or artificial material and sized to meet your needs; or a pit blind below the ground that allows you to be concealed better compared to an above ground blind.

Natural material is by far the best camo covering. If, for example, you are hunting in a field that once consisted of standing corn, the corn stalk residue would be excellent for concealment. Both ducks and geese are attracted to cut corn, rye, bean, and similar crop fields. If you know a farmer who will leave a few rows of standing crops (especially corn), you will have an excellent natural blind setting.

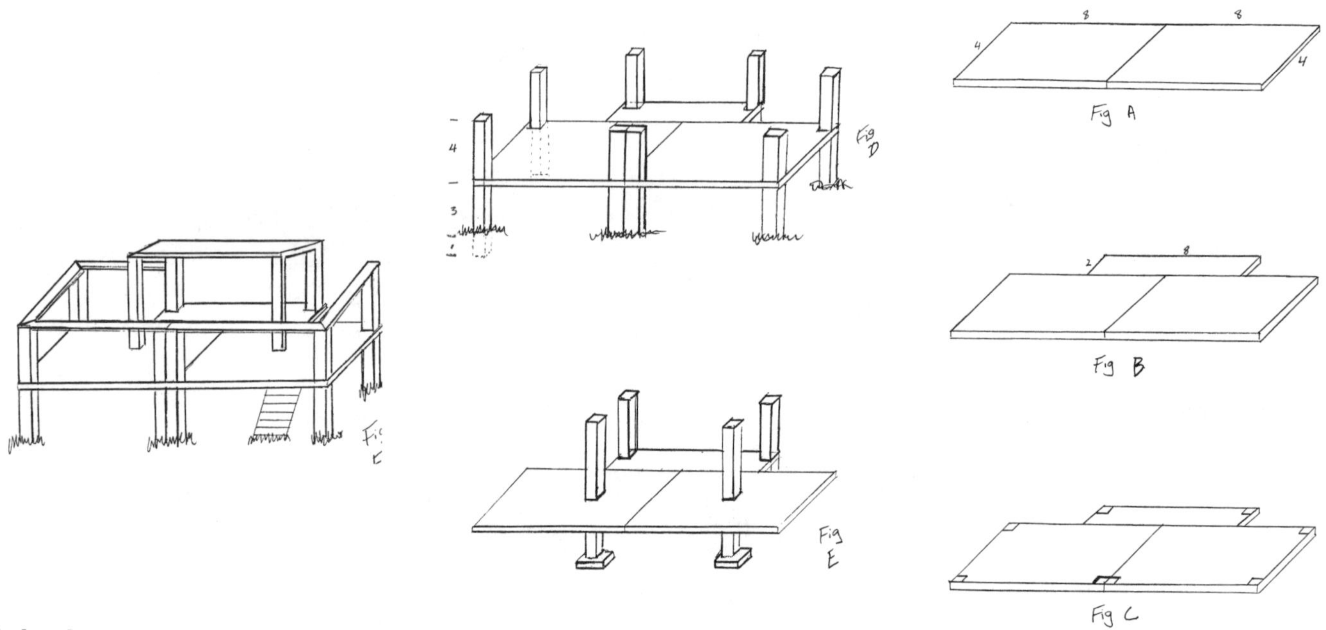

John Lee
Mineola, TX

Stationary Duck Blind

A large blind that will hunt at least 3-4 people. Constructed during the dry summer period and used when the water level comes up during the waterfowl season.

Construction Notes: Start with two sheets of 3/4 inch marine plywood, nailed to 2 x 4 wolmanized wood frame on 16 inch centers. Next add a 2 x 8 foot extension on the back of the floor for added space. This extension is built the same way as the floor.

After the floor is finished, cut eight holes in the floor 4 x 4 inches for the leg supports. For the legs, use 4 x 4 x 8 wolmanized posts. The legs on this particular blind are installed approximately one foot deep into the ground. The floor is then attached to the legs with 16 penny nails, three feet above the ground.

Next add the two front supports for the roof. This is accomplished by cutting holes in the floor, and instead of placing the post inside the ground, place them on two cement blocks. This allows the two anterior posts to be one foot taller than the posterior posts, giving you a one foot fall on the roof from front to back. The roof measures 4 x 8 feet, and the top is covered with tar paper and shingled.

Following this procedure, connect all of the supporting legs on the top by making a hand rail of 2 x 4 inch wolmanized lumber. This is followed by nailing heavy duty galvanized field fence wire to the perimeter of the blind. This, along with adding support, will give you an ideal method of brushing the blind with natural surrounding vegetation.

Added features included a brush swinging gate with steps at the rear for entering; a dog ramp on the front left side; a bench for seating; and hangers along the walls for decoy bags, gun cases, and other accessories.

Greg Goda
Butler, PA

Metal Tubing Two-Person Frame Blind

A portable blind made from copper tubing, with partial top. Use in most any field situation, or along a shoreline or marsh.

Construction Notes: The corners are made by welding a piece of conduit that has the same inside dimension as the conduit outside dimension (approximately 3-4 inches long), vertically on each elbow. The bottom four corners are 90 degrees to the elbow. To make the different angles needed for the top corners, simply cut the end of the sections of pipe to the right angle and weld. If it is not exact, it doesn't matter. Measuring by eye is generally sufficient.

The conduit and elbows of the frame are bolted together with 1/8 inch bolts.

The roof supports are made of two pieces of 1 inch wide flat steel, drilled with a 1/4 inch hole in one end and a hole to accept a piece of conduit in the other end. The 1/4 inch bolts are soldered to conduit clamps and the conduit clamps are pop-riveted to the upper frame sides where the roof ends.

Paint does not stick well to the conduit, so you may consider covering it with brown contact paper or one of the camo tape coverings available on the market.

The final step is sewing the nylon cover. The brown camo material used on this blind came from a mail order house. It is 60 inches wide. The sizing of the covering can be accomplished by transferring the frame dimensions to a piece of graph paper, adding for seams and overlaps. From this, calculate the amount of material needed; in this case it is seven yards. The cloth is overlapped about three inches over the top so it will not sag, and then held together with pieces of velcro. The bottom is held to the frame by sewing strips of velcro which are made by overlapping 1/4 inch of the ends of two pieces of velcro that are about 3 inches long. Sew these half to the nylon then looping the rest over the pipe.

Installing the cover over the frame is made easier by sewing a triangle of material on each of the upper corners, resulting in a pocket that keeps the cover from sliding to the ground before the velcro is fastened. Snaps could be used and would probably be faster to install, but will eventually rust.

One rear corner of the cover is left unsewn to be used for a door. It can be opened from the back or side as needed. These loose flaps are secured by loops of velcro, as is the bottom of the cover. The small inside flaps of the roof are kept from flapping in the wind by a couple of small pieces of velcro used to anchor the bottom of the flap to the rest of the blind.

One final touch is to sew strips of leftover cloth in 5-6 inch long sections to provide places to stick any available natural cover to break up the outline of the blind.

This entire framework and cover can be set up in the predawn hours by one person in less than five minutes using only a flashlight. The camo netting is placed over the frame along with some natural vegetation. A couple of pieces of 1/8 inch nylon cord is used as a tie down should high winds be prevalent.

Chip Fashner
Greenville, OH

Portable Blind on a Cart

Can be towed to your field hunting site, along with decoys, gun, and accessories. Use in any accessible field site or along a shoreline where it is possible to pull a cart.

Construction Notes: The floor, seat, and seat supports are made out of 3/4 inch plywood. The seat supports are hinged so they can be collapsed when not in use. The seat has 7/8 inch dado cuts so it can be placed on the uprights and firmly held in place (note: the uprights oppose each other in the way they fold to add extra stability when in use). The floor is covered with plastic backed trunk carpet.

The axle system detaches from the blind by removing four wing nuts and bolts that go through the floor of the blind. The tires are regular 15 inch lawn tractor tires. The handle is 3/4 inch conduit that is hinged, and detaches by removing 4 pins and snap clips. All of the pipe used on the blind frame is one inch, schedule 80 PVC for lightweight and durability. The bottom section of the PVC is permanently attached to the floor and glued together to give a small railing to hold gear and other items. The drawings will depict other areas that the blind comes apart for storage and transportation.

The camouflage is cordura with Leaf-o-flage windows and a front shooting lid. The back and side camo is attached permanently to the back upper rail, and the side supports to the first break joint. It only requires one place (on each side of the front) for the camo to be fastened during set up. This is the area on the front of the blind where it wraps around. Because this is covered by the front piece of camo lid, it can be achieved with two large bag ties. The one side has a door, which is slit cut in the material that is held together by velcro with a storm flap also sewed on. The front camo lid with the two pipes sewn in lies over the blind; one pipe hanging over the back, and the second at the front of the side upper rail. It is then fastened with four velcro straps, two on each side to secure it from blowing in the wind. This entire front assembly is like a pit lid that is thrown open when it is time to shoot. The camo has two weeding strings sewn lengthwise, one on the front and one on each side to help hold cattails, corn stalks, or other natural covering.

The blind weighs approximately 45 pounds, and will carry up to 5 dozen field shells. It is designed to slide in and out of the back of a pick-up truck without any need to dissemble and it takes no more than 15 minutes to have this completely set-up and covered. Four hunters can handle it comfortably.

Material List:

Blind Frame:
(100 feet) Schedule 80 (1 inch)PVC
(14) 'T's
(7) Crosses
(5) 45 degree angles
(6) 90 degree angles
(note: all couplings are schedule 80)
(12) 1 inch conduit straps

Handle:
(8 feet) 3/4 inch conduit
(2) conduit hinges
(4) 1/4 inch bolts and nuts
(4 feet) 1/2 inch steel pipe
(2) 2-1/2 inch muffler clamps
(4) 1/2 inch bolts and wing nuts
(4) 1/4 inch pins and snap clips

Seat & Floor:
(1) 2 x 4
(2 sheets) 3/4 inch cdx plywood
(8) hinges
(1) 4 x 8 sheet of plastic trunk carpet
Approximately 70 (2 inch) drywall screws

Camouflage:
10 yards of Cordura camo
10 x 8 foot piece of Leaf-o-flage
3 feet of Velcro (1/2 inch wide)
Paint (1/2 gallon)
(25) plastic wire holders

Axle Assembly:
(2) 15 inch lawn tractor tires
(8 feet) 1/2 x 1 inch sq steel tubing

Jeff Wright
Grand Rapids, OH

Simple Roll-up Field Blind

Easy to construct portable blind for one person. Use in fields, along a pond or river, or in a marsh.

Construction Notes: Construction of this portable blind is very easy, and can be accomplished in a few hours with materials found at a local hardware or building supply store.

Material List:
*(14 feet) 36 inch chicken wire
*(6-8) 4-1/2 foot (1-1/4 inch) wood dowels
*100 foot roll of binder twine (brown)
*small fencing staples and marsh grass

Start by determining the length of the blind you wish to construct. Fourteen feet works well in most cases for two hunters and a dog. This size will also cover the side of a small hunting boat. Next cut bundles of grass from your hunting site, separate into small bundles about the diameter of a quarter and tie in two or three places with twine. When a pile of stalks has accumulated, it's time to attach these to the wire mesh. Make sure the end you start with is square and weave the stalks in and out of the holes 4-5 times until you reach the bottom. Continue until you have reached the desired length. Pay special attention to keeping the stalks perpendicular to the top.

When the grass has all been woven into the mesh, attach two of your dowels, one at each end. Use fencing staples, securing them well. The remaining dowels are unattached as they can be woven into the mesh wherever they will best accommodate the shape desired. When rolled up to transport, one dowel can be woven in to hold the blind together.

A.J. Vogelsberg
Fisherville, KY

Metal Pit Blind

An 8 x 8 x 16 foot pit blind constructed with a combination of steel from a tractor-trailer floor, treated lumber, and includes room for two retrievers.

Construction Notes: This pit blind gives up to five hunters plenty of head room to move around inside, and with two (55 gallon) drums, provides space for two retrievers.

Two 4 x 8 sheets of steel from the floor of a tractor-trailer were used for the walls. Frames are made out of treated 2 x 4's after which you lag-screw the steel to the frames. A backhoe operator took about an hour and a half to dig the hole, making sure it is wide enough to work in; be sure to include wide slopes around the entire hole to prevent caving. The pit is equipped with a 12 volt lighting system, sump pump, and propane stove for heat. Depending on where you are placing this type of blind, be sure to take into consideration the amount of groundwater that can seep into the pits. It is well worth the time to include a sump or other type of bailing system.

Material List:
(60) 2 x 4s, each eight feet long
(9) 2 x 6s, each eight feet long
(5) 2 x 6s, each twelve feet long
(1) 2 x 10, sixteen feet long
(1) 2 x 6, sixteen feet long
(2) 2 x 4s, sixteen feet long
128 square feet of 1 x 6 inch sheeting for floor
96 square feet of half-inch plywood for roof
96 square feet of galvanized metal for roof
(note: 4 x 8 sheets of steel can be replaced with plywood, but will add to the expense)

Jeff Rud
Madison, SD

Bale Blind

A unique "bale blind" constructed with twine, resembling a hay bale commonly seen in farm country. Will accommodate two hunters and folds down to less than a foot in height. Can be transported in a pickup truck.

Construction Notes: Construction of this blind starts by cutting equal lengths of 3/4 inch rollpipe approximately 16 feet long. This will give a bale size five feet in diameter. Cut the lengths extra long or leave on the roll to determine the size needed. Ream the 3/4 inch PVC "T" fittings so that they just slip over the 3/4 inch roll pipe. This is key to allowing the blind to fold.

Slide all the 3/4 inch "T"s necessary for the side braces, cross braces, and the foot supports onto the roll pipe. Construct two wheels using the "T" 3/4 inch PVC fittings to make the supports for the wheels. When complete and fully round, use the 3/4 inch rollpipe inside as butt splices to complete the sides. Use PVC cement on all joints except those contacting the roll pipe.

Next the horizontal supports can be glued, making them 1/2 the width of the blind so they can fold to the center of the wheels. Cut the one inch PVC pipe long enough to support the horizontal pieces, but short enough so that they can be slipped off on the side.

Drill a hole through the foot pieces, install the electric posts and use the hose clamps to fasten the posts to the side support pieces. The blind should stand on its own and fold flat when disassembled.

Cut and sew the burlap tightly on the frame, making sure it is tight when open. Other materials besides twine or burlap can be used depending on your hunting area. Viewing slits can be cut where needed.

Cut the blind handles so they rest on the sides of the blind, except the bottom one which will fit into the "T" fitting. Sew the broomsticks onto the burlap and cover with twine. The door of broom handles will collapse when pushed open to provide excellent shooting visibility. The entire door can be removed to provide easier access.

Material List:
(40) feet of 3/4 inch plastic pipe (roll type)
(2) 3/4 inch inside butt splices for pipe
(1) can of PVC cement
(70) feet of 3/4 inch PVC pipe;
ten foot lengths
(40) 3/4 inch PVC "T" fittings
(2) 3/4 inch PVC "T" fittings
(20) feet of one inch PVC pipe;
must slip over 3/4 inch pipe
(4) electric fence posts
(8) 1-1/2 inch hose clamps
(5) broom handles; 5/8 inch diameter
(20) sq yards of burlap
(1) bale of sisal twine

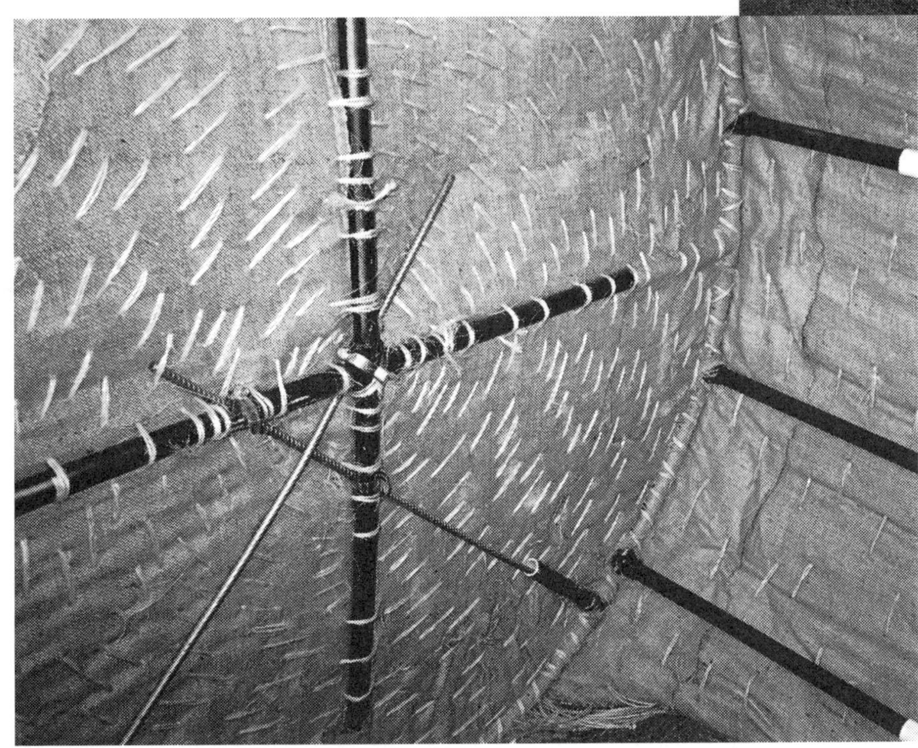

Henry Nelson
Athens, GA

Portable Field Blind Framework

A simple, portable, lightweight field blind for one or two people, utilizing a natural or synthetic camo covering. Can be used along a shoreline, in a shallow-water marsh, or open field.

Construction Notes: The wood used to construct this blind is western cedar, however pine can also be used. The back panel is 8 x 8 feet; front panel is 8 x 7 feet. Both are covered with chicken wire or light gauge fence to support vegetation covering. The corners of the blind are connected with carriage bolts (4 x 1/4 inch). A 2 x 2 is attached approximately three quarters of the way up from the base to allow the hunters to push against when ready to shoot, allowing the blind to collapse.

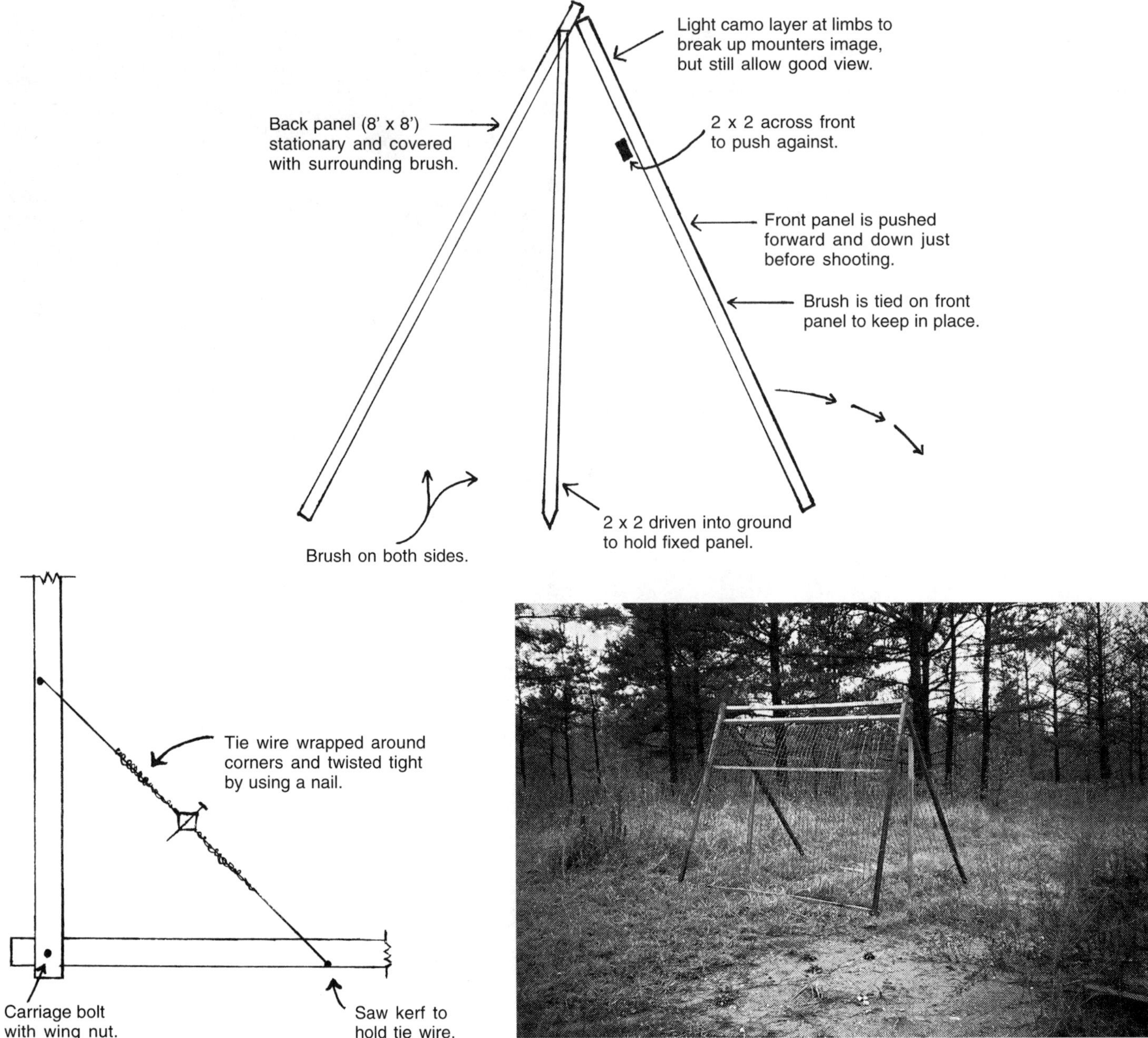

Dick Schumacher
Kearney, NE

The Goosebuster Field Blind

A versatile mobile field blind that is towed to and from hunting locations. Used anywhere a field blind can be towed, including next to a lake, river, or pond.

Construction Notes: The Goosebuster is a portable, mobile blind capable of hunting two people, and has an optional dog kennel. It can be set up in 10 minutes, camouflaged to your personal taste, and relatively inexpensive to construct. The unit doubles as a storage for decoys and other duck hunting stuff.

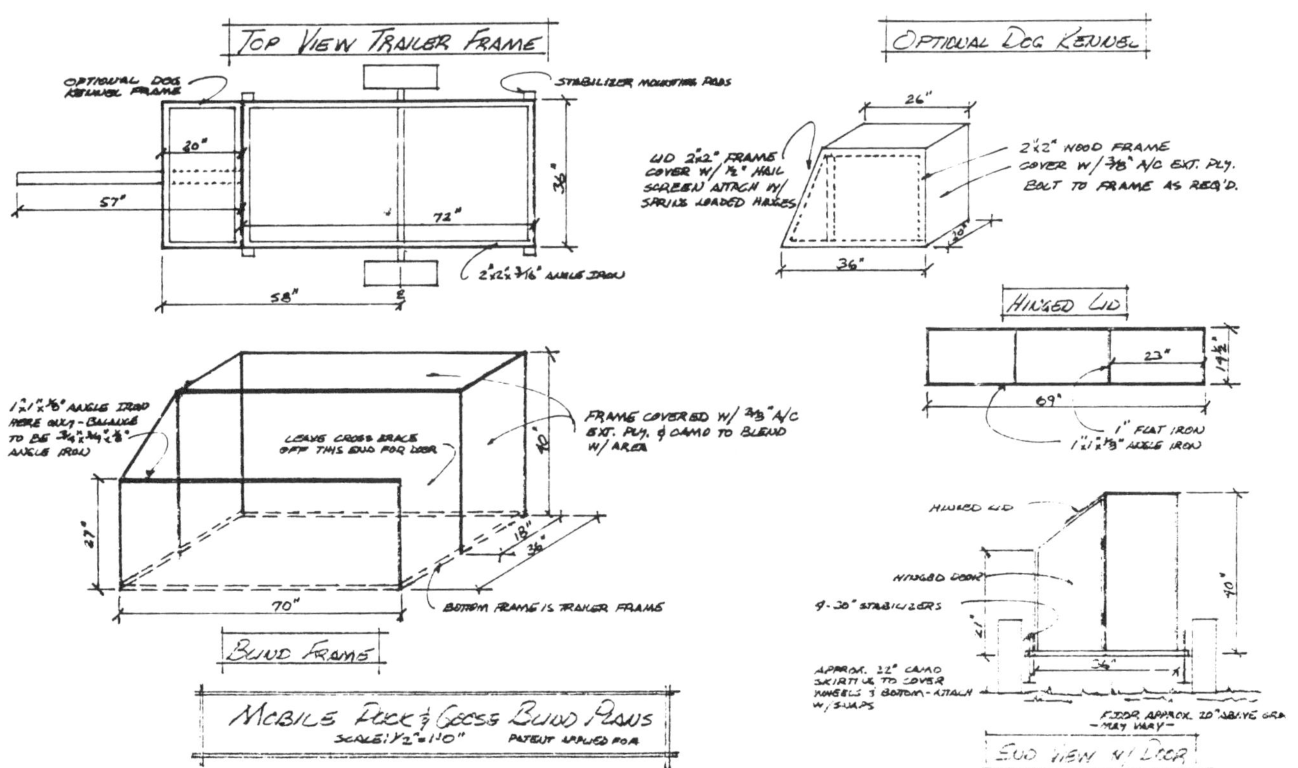

Ed Cummings
Somonauk, IL

Improved Coffin Blind

Take a conventional coffin blind and make it more "user friendly".

Construction Notes: The first feature is the top frame support legs that fold flat for storage and transport, dropping down and locking in place to support the top frame when in use. All framework for this blind, including the folding legs, are made of 2 x 4's cut down to 1-1/8 thick by 2 inches wide. This gives adequate strength without excessive weight. No particular dimensions are given because the builder can make it to fit their own needs.

To make the legs work properly, the blind should be built complete, excluding the top covers. To accomplish this, support the top frame in position with temporary support blocks until the blind is complete and covered with your choice of material. When this part is complete, determine where you want your legs and follow the diagram. A bolt size of 5/16 or 3/8 inch work well.

Next, determine the length of the leg you need and drill it on center to accept the bushing. The bushing I.D. should be as close as possible to the bolt diameter so it allows the leg to swing freely, but not allow too much slop. Make the bushing approximately 1/8 inch longer than the thickness of the leg and allow about 1/16 inch to extend on each side of the leg. Cut the bottom of the leg about 1/2 inch above, and parallel to, the blind floor. Attach the piece of 10 gauge to the bottom edge of the leg. Attach the leg to the blind and tighten the locknut just enough to keep the leg straight, but still moving freely.

Make the bottom latch plate of 10 gauge steel. It is made of two separate pieces including the top piece which acts as a guide and latch, and the bottom piece which keeps the leg from tearing up the floor. With all legs attached and latch plates made, slide the latch plates under the legs to locate them and determine the proper tension on the side covering.

Don't set the legs too tight, leave about 1/8 to 1/4 inch of slack to allow for easy disassembly.

When all the legs are in place and adjusted, remove the temporary supports by lifting up on the pairs of legs at each end, and releasing them. The blind will now collapse. To erect, grab the top frame near the center and lift up. The legs will now drop down and lock in position.

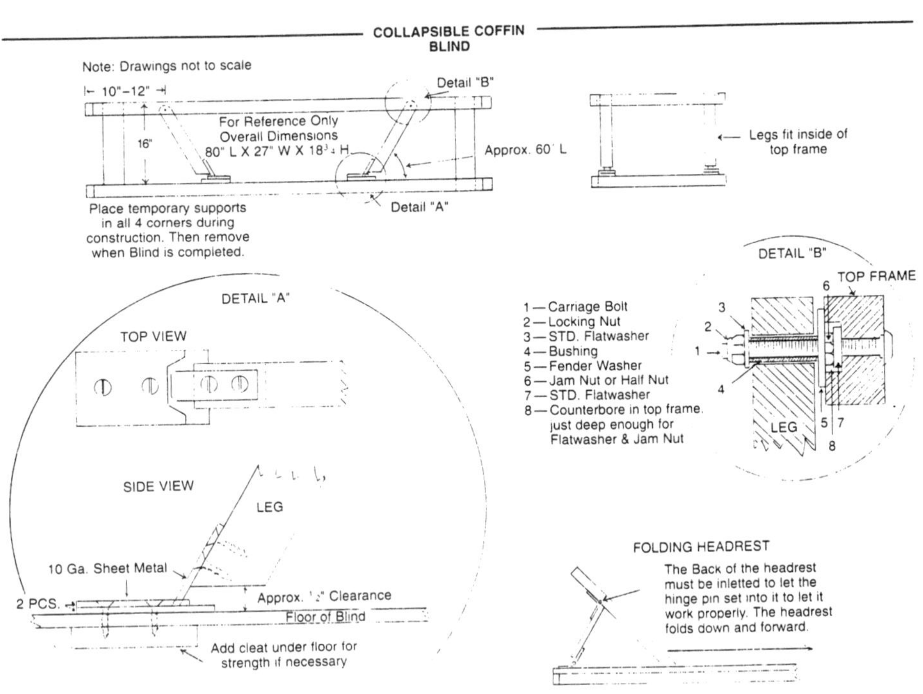

The second feature with this design is the lid. The lid frames are made in two sections from PVC pipe. The portion over the feet is hinged, whereas the portion over the body is not. Make the body portion of the lid big enough so you are able to stand straight and shoot without having to scoot forward to get in this position.

Both lids are held closed with 3/4 inch velcro with adhesive backing. These are cut to 3 inch lengths. A 1/8 inch pop rivet is used at each end to help secure the velcro.

The feet portion of the lid has one piece of velcro on the side opposite the hinges. The body portion of the lid is held by a strip of velcro on each side at the center, allowing the user to slide the lid down to watch for birds and to cover up quickly with minimal movement.

When birds approach, release the Velcro® gently and the lid can be pushed down towards the feet or slid off either side. This is especially convenient when the birds are not exactly where you want them to be, or the wind is coming from the wrong direction for a hinged lid. More often than not, according to the designer of this blind, waterfowl (especially geese), will not notice the lid being opened until it is too late.

Another feature of this lid is a window to view out when the lid is completely closed. This window is covered with black fiberglass screen and allows you to see out, but not let working birds to see you. It is velcro latched on the inside.

Another feature is a folding headrest. You must cut a slot in the back side of the headrest so the hinge pin can fit into it and allow the hinge to work properly.

Before attaching the hinges, remove the hinge pins and bend them slightly. This provides enough friction for the headrest to remain in position for use, but still allows it to fold down. Use a 1 x 6 for the support and a 1 x 12 for the headrest. The hinges are 3 inch butt hinges.

A rope handle is attached at each end of the base for easy transporting. Three small rope "eyes" on each side of the base are used to attach bungee cords for securing during storage or transportation. The blind is covered with canvas from an old tent. Painting of the canvas will depend on the habitat you intend to use this blind in.

Milton Nehrke
Bath, NY

"Cow" Field Blind

A portable silhouette blind used when hunting cow pastures; often a site for incoming flocks of geese and sometimes ducks. Use this blind in any "friendly" cow pasture.

Construction Notes: Here are basically two methods of constructing this particular blind: 1) Free hand an outline of a cow on a sheet of plywood, or 2) Find a friendly cow and have her lay down on a 4 x 8 sheet of plywood, thereby sketching her outline.

Besides a hide for the hunter, the advantages of this blind are many:

- Wildfowl show no fear of cattle and regularly land within easy shooting range.
- The blind can easily be built in a variety of sizes, accommodating a single hunter (Calf model), two hunter model (Cow), three hunters (Bull model), four hunters (Magnum Bull model), or surprise model (Trojan Cow).
- Some hunters will ask about the problem of those birds that pass over and return from behind the hunter. This is not a problem since at that time the hunter merely rests his/her shotgun against the, uh... (cow) blind, and pretend to be milking the cow. This strategy however, does not work well with the bull model.
- One could expand the basic confidence decoy method of placing a plastic cat next to the cow, a rubber teat squirting milk at the cat, and a tail that swishes and hits the hunter in the back of the head.

Fred Quinterno
Nevada, CA

Field Cart

A (deer) field cart transformed into a field hunting rig used to transport decoys and other gear to and from your hunting site.

Construction Notes: After purchasing this unit, spray paint it a camo color, and extend the straps to accommodate the field decoys (up to six dozen). It also has a strap that goes around your neck so you can rest your arms without setting the rig down. Not a bad method of getting all your gear from point 'A' to point 'B' especially if you're alone.

John Molkenbur
White Bear Lake, MN

Trailer Blind

I'm not sure where White Bear Lake, MN is located, but it sounds like a place that is a hunters' dream; numerous unnamed lakes filled with bass, trout and panfish, old fencelines and brush-chocked two-tracks supporting an abundance of ringnecks, and of course bountiful waterfowl habitat. "The Willow Wagon" is basically a utility trailer with a simple camo blind designed to fit the top portion. If you have a trailer and hunt open fields, this may work for you.

Construction Notes: This particular blind is made on a 5 x 8 trailer, large enough for three hunters. The blind is constructed using roughly 42 feet of 3/4 inch electrical conduit pipe. The physical dimensions of the trailer include 2 sides (8 x 2 foot), 2 ends (5 x 2 foot), and 4 uprights (4 x 4 foot). Use 8 (45 degree) end connectors for joining all the conduit. Drill out four of the end pieces in order for the pipe to pass through. You will also need eight eyehooks: slide the 3/4 inch pipe into the hooks to hold in place.

Camouflage with whatever works for you (e.g. burlap, willow, grass mats, artificial camo, corn stalks), add seats and whatever else you may want, and tow to your favorite field location. Slick!

Field blinds can be as simple as digging a shallow hole with a small shovel and covering up with a natural or artificial covering material as shown in this photo of Michigan waterfowler Steve Armstrong hunting near Quanicassee, Michigan.

When using a pit blind, be sure to place several decoys around your pit as shown here.

A seat type pit blind allows the hunter to get a better view of incoming birds, and generally is more comfortable as shown here in this northern Texas cut crop field.

Hauling all your gear out to your hunting site can be easily accomplished by obtaining a set of wheels and constructing a box to carry all your gear.

~ 2 ~
Shore Blinds

Sitting in a stand of cattail along the shore of a lake or bay is the easiest and most effective blind you can find.

In the absence of a natural camo cover, a simple artificial blind will provide adequate cover as long as the hunter remains still until the final second before shooting. A blind with 360 degree sides and at least a partial top will be even more effective.

Utilizing a coffin-type blind close to the shoreline on a lake, river or pond works great on puddle or diver ducks.

Benny Bechtol
Oklahoma City, OK

Portable Shore Blind

A 4 x 8 foot blind built primarily for a marsh or body of water that has a relatively flat or slightly sloping bottom, but can easily be moved in or out, due to the unique "feet" design if water conditions change. Also used as a land blind near a body of water. Will fit onto a trailer or truck with a four-foot bed.

Construction Notes: The sides of this blind were built from discarded stockade fencing that was old and weathered. One quarter inch holes are drilled through the runners into the floor and framework, and the sides are then pinned to the frame with 1/4 x 8 inch carriage bolts (no nut necessary). There are six in the front and back and four on the sides. A hinged opening is designed into the back of the blind near the center. Since most hunters will, at one time or another, have a dog in the blind, a couple of ramps complete with their own hinged doors could also be built into the blind design. The ramps and doors are attached to the feet by a small chain.

Leaf-o-flage is attached to the Z-Frame with 3/4 x 9 inch lengths of conduit and is held in place over the blind opening with curtain rod holders. Reed grass, brush or other suitable cover can be tied around the blind as needed.

A couple of 10 foot long pipes (2 inch diameter) are placed under the framework next to the 4 x4 legs for lifting the blind to or from a particular location. Four men can easily move the blind. Buoyancy helps once it is in the water. This blind is 8 feet from the feet to the overhang, 8 feet long, and 4 feet deep.

Material List:
*Feet: (2) 3 foot x 12 inch x 9 inch matting boards or bridge timbers
*Legs: (4) 4 x 4 inch x 8 foot treated posts
*Floor: (24) 2 x 4 inch x 4 foot (or any width) 2 inch boards
*Frame: 32 feet of 2 x 6s and 32 feet of 2 x 4s
*Sides: (3) 8 foot panels of 6 foot stockade fencing
*Top:(2) 2 x 10 inch x 8 foot wood shingles or brown asphalt
*(2) 2 x 2-1/2 inch x 3 foot for ramp opening
*(1) 2 x 4 inch x 6 foot bracing
*Doors: (1) 1 x 4 inch x 6 foot bracing
*(1) 3/8 inch x 4 x 4 foot plywood (door backing)
*Dog Ramps: (2) 2 x 12 inch x 5 foot & (1) 1 x 2 inch x 6 foot (steps)

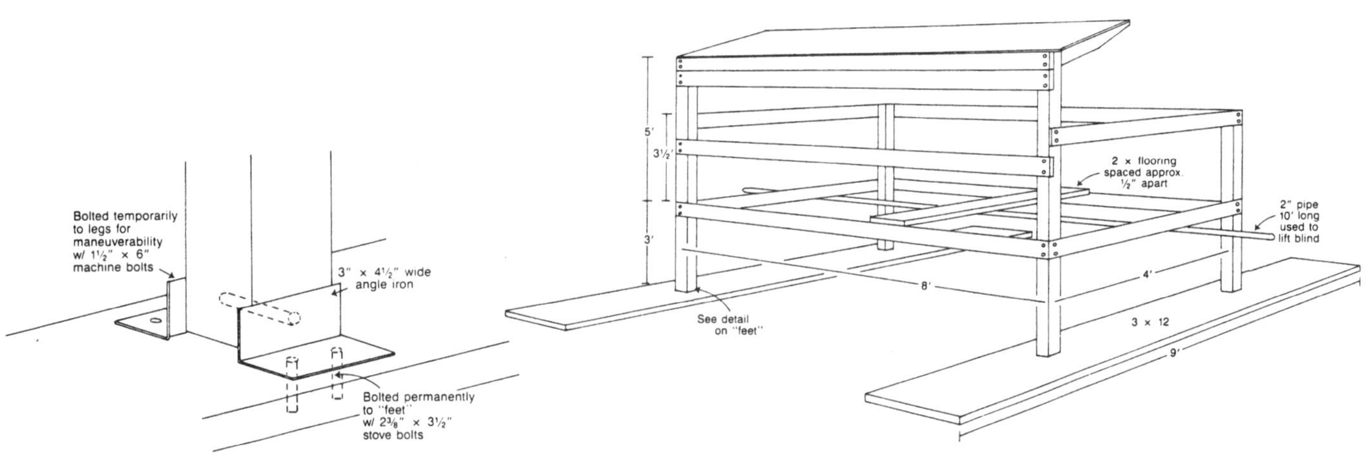

A permanent shore blind constructed of metal or wood and brushed, is idea if the area you hunt allows for such a blind.

Mike Dearth & Company
Coal City, IL

Concrete "bunker" Style Blind

If you want durability, this is it; a 12 x 12 foot "blind" complete with sleeping area and kitchen, and constructed with 13,000 pounds (3-1/2 yards) of concrete.

Construction Notes: The extreme weight of concrete created problems for the designers of this unique blind. Therefore panels were made using forms allowing each panel to be no more than 2 feet wide and 2-1/4 inches thick. This allows 4-5 people to handle them relatively safely. Since the area that the blind was to be constructed is only accessible by boat, each section had to be handled by hand without the benefit of machinery.

The size of this blind (12 x 12) allow for enough space for a 6 x 12 combination back room/kitchen, and a equal size shooting area. The ceiling is 6 feet 5 inches. Taking into consideration the size of the blind and the weight, 40 separate panels are used (2 feet wide x 6 feet-4 inches high).

Each of the panels weigh approximately 355 pounds. All the concrete used was specially designed high cement content concrete to compensate for only being 2-1/2 inches thick. Wire mesh is added to every panel for strength.

Two by six treated boards are laid down as a level footing for the panels. A pontoon boat is used to transport the panels to the blind location.

The back of the blind is constructed first by bolting each panel together with 5-1/2 x 3/8 inch bolts and 2 x 4 foot boards. The holes for the bolts are made by using 1/2 inch PVC, nailed in place to leave a hole when the concrete is poured around it. Each corner is bolted together using 8 x 1 inch steel strap, pre-bent in a 90 degree angle. After the entire blind is built the roof is then lifted on. Between each 9 foot section, a 2-1/2 inch "H" beam was used for the panels to fit into. This gave the roof extra support. After the roof panels are completed, a layer of tar, black paper, tar, and another layer of paper is applied to insure weather proofing. The entire blind is covered with soil.

The blind is landscaped to blend in with the surrounding area. Cracks are caulked with tar, the kitchen is painted white for brightness, benches and a table is made for the kitchen, a four burner stove added, and mouse proof shelving for food. The shooting area is painted a dark brown and 2 x 6 inch treated planks were cut for the floor. Wood is used for the shooting area because it would be warmer than concrete. The concrete in the back kitchen area worked well because it is easier to keep clean.

Once the hole was dug, it took three weekends to construct the blind. Hard work? Absolutely. Worth it? You bet.

Don Mattice
Saratoga Springs, NY

Location is Everything

This blind is located on a lake that attracts ducks year after year. A spot that is calm even on days when freighter captains look for sheltered bays and harbors. Not only is this area calm, easy to locate, but also has a hard sandy bottom with enough water to float a good sized boat, but shallow enough to set out decoys in his waders.

Construction Notes: The base of the blind is constructed of 2 x 4s; 12 inches on center with 3/4 inch plywood sheathing. The front, back, sides and roof are framed from rough cut 2 x 3s. Half-inch plywood sheathing was nailed to the outside. The roof is weatherproofed with fiberglass rolled roofing material. The removable panels are made from 1/2 inch plywood sheathing attached to an inside frame of 2 x 2s. The panels are fastened inside with eye hooks, placed on the inside of the panels to make them easier to remove and put back up after the hunt.

The front, back, roof, base, and side sections are prefabricated. Three coats of good quality, solid color stain are used to seal out moisture. The stain is applied to the frame and sheathing before fabrication to assure all wood surfaces were treated. A gray color is chosen in this case to blend with the natural surrounding habitat. Dark brown on the inside works well to help conceal movement within the blind.

Once the sections are transported to the hunting site, the base is positioned on a solid piece of ground. The front, back, and sides are then fastened together and to the base with hex head lag bolts. Flat washers are used to prevent the bolts from being drawn too deeply into the frame. The roof is attached to the walls with framing brackets. All brackets and lag bolt heads are painted with flat black spray paint to eliminate glare. For added stability, wooden stakes are driven into the ground and nailed to the base of the blind. Add some leafy brush to the front of the blind before each season, and you have a blind that will serve you well for years.

The only thing that this author would like to know is the GPS coordinates of the blind.

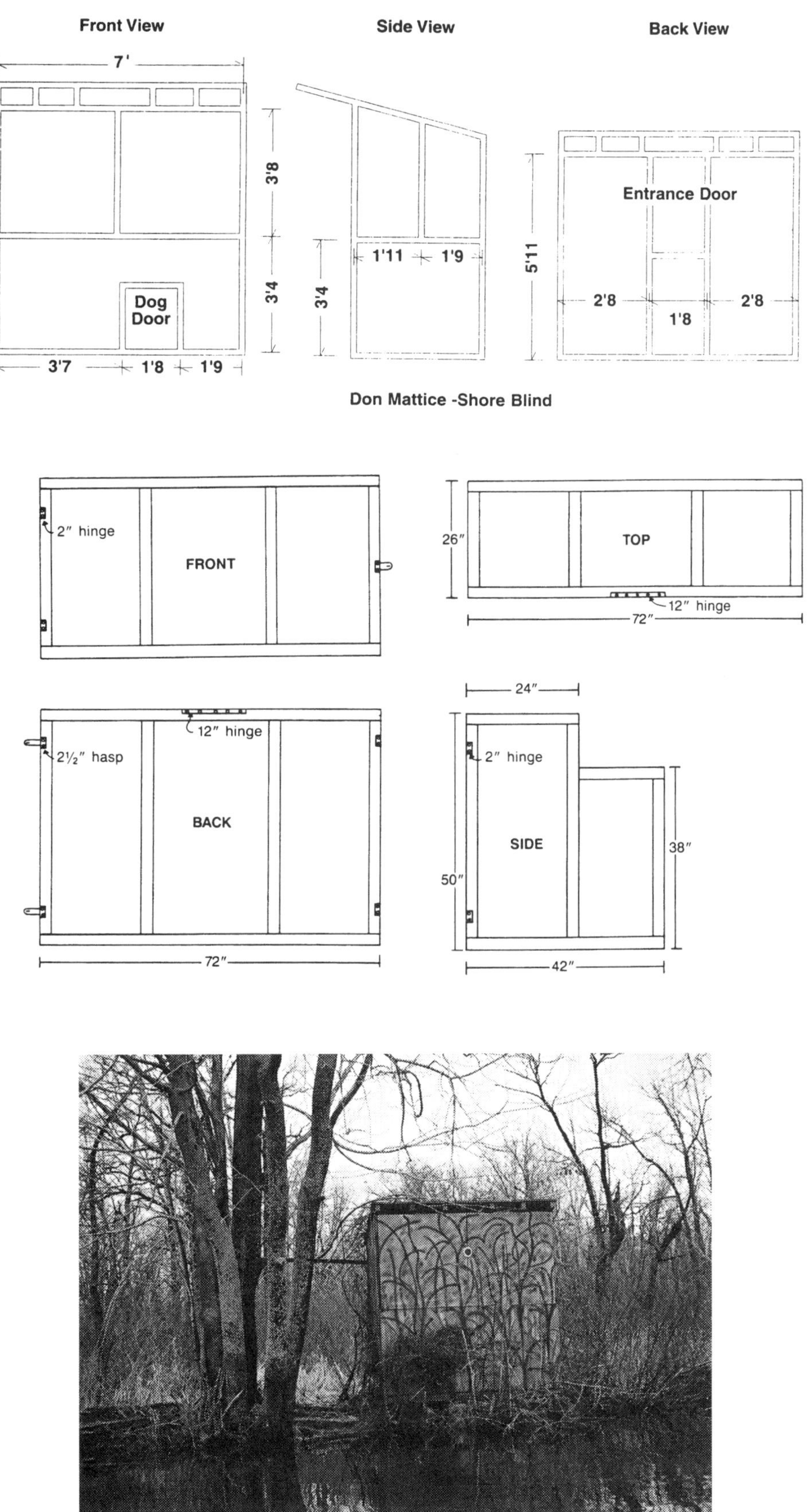

Don Mattice -Shore Blind

~ 3 ~
Johnboats

Dennis Nickless
Bloomington, IN

Fourteen Foot Johnboat with Blind

A removable blind frame made with half-inch & three-quarter inch conduit.

Construction Notes: The blind frame is made mainly of 1/2 inch conduit, with 3/4 inch used at certain high stress points. The main frame pieces are setting on the three boat seats. These three (3/4") pieces lay the entire width of the seat and then turn up and back over towards the center of the boat. Sections of 1/2 inch conduit are then welded in place the entire length of the boat. The frame is secured to the seats with conduit straps screwed to the seats. The right side of the frame is solid the entire length of the boat, while the left side has a door opening. The flaps are made of 1/2 inch conduit and each one is hinged to the main frame. The flaps are hinged. The frame and flaps can be covered with thin, pliable 4 or 5 inch fencing. Use plastic tie wraps to fasten the burlap. Paint the frame and flaps before covering.

Most blinds do not provide for a covered top for overhead flyers, but with this design you are 90 percent hidden. There are pieces of burlap attached to the flaps to cover openings in the top. Surgical tubing is stretched the entire length of the boat on the main frame and flaps to attach a natural vegetation (i.e. reed grass, cattail, corn stalks). The tubing is elastic, strong, and is attached every two feet to the boat.

The flaps lie down on the main frame during boating or when being transported. The back flaps (right side of boat), are up in a more vertical position while the front (shooting side) are lower to allow a good view of incoming birds. When birds start to drop in, push the front flaps down and shoot from a sitting or standing position. Retrievers can easily climb over the side to retrieve downed birds, and entering once again at the transom.

Material List:
1/2 and 3/4 inch thinwall conduit
1/4 inch sheet metal screws
Tiewraps or strong string
Burlap covering
Olive drab/black/brown paint
Surgical tubing
Lightweight 4 or 5 inch square fence
Welded apparatus for thin metal
Conduit bender

Marty Modrowski, Sr.
Toledo, OH

Welded Frame Blind on 14 Foot Fishing Boat

A welded thin wall metal frame blind made with 1/2 and 3/4 inch conduit. Fencing (2-1/4 x 2-1/4 inch) and canvas complete the main materials. It is attached to the gunwales with ten mineriallac connectors (electrical fastener) which are held in place with 1/4 inch bolts. Can be attached or removed in twenty minutes. Has three access doors and three roof sections that are easily able to pop open.

Construction Notes: First fasten the mineriallac connectors to the gunwale of your boat every two feet. Next attach 1/2 inch conduit to those connectors. Use a propane torch to heat the conduit after you have it in place in order for it to take a set. Use a conduit bender for any sharp bends. After you have the bottom frame complete, your next move is to construct the top opening. When you have the top opening complete, you will need an extra set of hands to hold the top in place while you get corner supports in place. After the corner supports are attached, you start at any location to install the remaining supports. Supports are not coped in. One inch of each end of the support is hammered flat, then trimmed to fit.

Next make your doors to fit your openings. Doors should fit over your door frames. The sketch will show you how to make the hinges out of banding. Try to make the roof sections as equal as possible. When the roof is complete, determine where you want to place your top rail trusses. These are necessary to keep your frame from spreading. Consider locating them so that the center roof section is resting above these trusses.

To make the roof hinges, take pieces of 6 inch pipe and cut them in half lengthwise. These will go around the top rail and welded back together. Take blank hinges and cut them so they are one inch wide. Half of the hinge is welded to the 6 inch pipe, the other half welded to the roof section. There should be nine sets of hinges on each side of the top rail. Each roof section should have three sets of hinges per side, six sets per section.

Cut the fence wire two lengths longer than you need in order to use the extra length to wrap around the supports. This will help hold the wire in place. Each section is custom fitted. Do not install the wire too tight as it will twist the frame. Also, do not cover the top rail. Leave space open between the top rail and the first support (sides only) to allow for a good viewing area.

Cut the canvas long enough to roll at least half way around the conduit. Then, using contact cement, attach the canvas to the frame. At this point, use wire ties to hold the canvas on at hard to hold spots. Fill any holes in the canvas.

To make the "top pop", drill thru the center support of each roof section. Eye bolts should be located in the middle of each section. Take a rubber tie down cord (hooks attached), and stretch it from the eye bolt to the gunwale. Correct length will hold the roof closed, but will also pop the top with a slight head pressure on the way up to shoot, or with minimal hand pressure.

The last step is to place the 18 inch wire on the outside of the canvas. Use the wire ties to accomplish this. Don't use more than necessary. All wire should take less than 50 of the ties to hold secure. This wire is used to hold your natural vegetation.

Material List:

*150 feet of 1/2 inch thin wall conduit
*13 feet of 3/4 inch thin wall conduit
*40 feet of 2-1/4 x 2-1/2 inch fence wire (vinyl covered), four-feet wide
*30 feet of same size fence wire, 18 inches wide
*100 wire ties (large enough to go around 1/2 inch conduit)
*45 feet of canvas, four feet wide
*18 (4 inch) blank hinges (roof hinges)
*18 (6 inch) long pieces of 3/4 inch pipe (roof)
*3 feet banding (door hinges)
*3 eye bolts (roof)
*12 (1/2 inch) conduit holders (mineriallac connectors)
*12 (1/4 inch) nuts, bolts, lock washers
*1 quart of quality contact cement

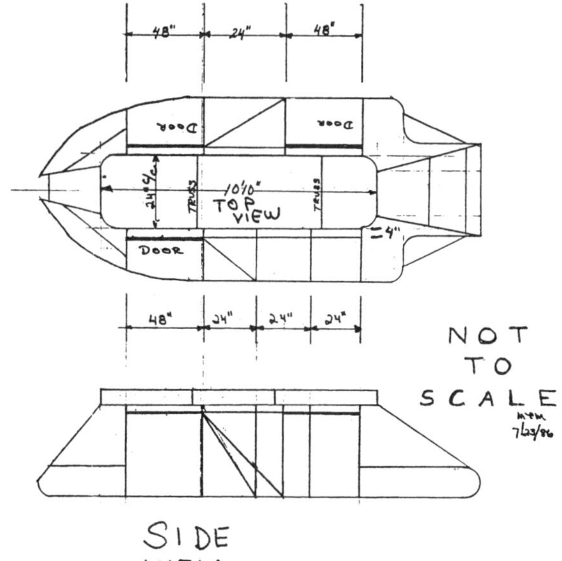

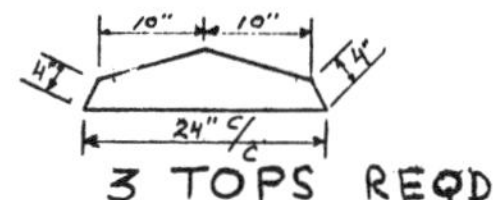

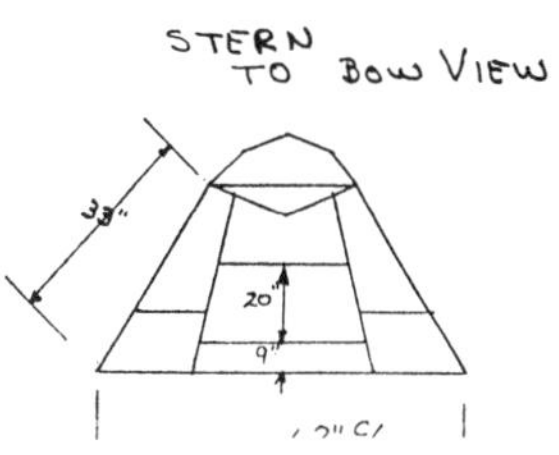

Michael Eckery
Lincoln, NE

Broom Corn Frame Blind

This blind is constructed on a 16 foot Lowe (Big John). It is supported by a framework of electrical conduit welded at the joints and corners. A cover of extremely thin aluminum sheeting (.016 inch) is popriveted to the framework. Light gauge fencing is attached and stalks of broom corn woven into place. Broom corn is used because its flexibility allows the rig to be towed at highway speeds with little or no wind damage. The blind can be easily removed from the boat by loosening a few bolts.

Construction Notes: The front deck serves as the entrance to the blind. The platform ladder allows your retriever to easily enter and is strong enough to be helpful to hunters as well. The hinged deck cover hides the deck and front door area while hunting.

Water from dogs or hunters drips onto the carpeted deck, then runs into a channel that drains out the side of the boat. A piece of aluminum channel attached to the back side of the front deck serves as a drainage gutter. The original bench seats were removed and replaced with adjustable height pedestal seats, allowing hunters a better seating arrangement.

Two radiant heaters and a propane stove were added for comfort, and padded gun racks for safe gun storage. Along the port and back side are larger shelves for each hunter's personal gear. The aluminum shelves are mounted on piano hinges and supported by a fine steel cable. Each shelf can be folded up flat against the side wall for extra internal space. The opening at the rear of the blind can be covered to prevent heat loss.

The cover is attached to the top and seals with Velcro on the side edges. Pleats allow the cover to expand, and yet stay in place when the motor is fully tilted. When access to the motor is needed, the cover simply lays over the top of the blind. A short piece of dark colored garden hose has been slit and glued to the edge of the blind to prevent scratching gun barrels.

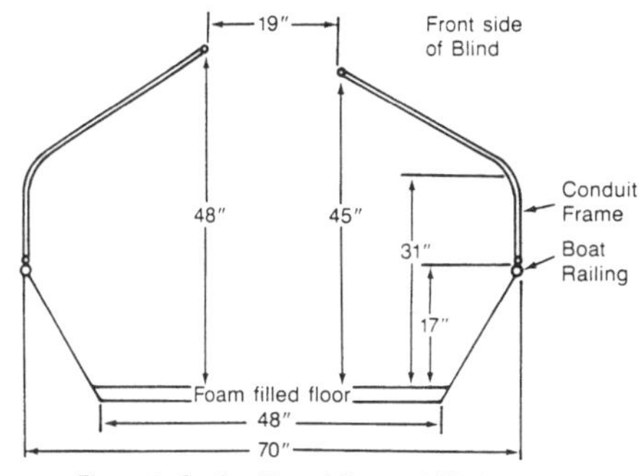

Figure 1. Section View of Boat and Blind

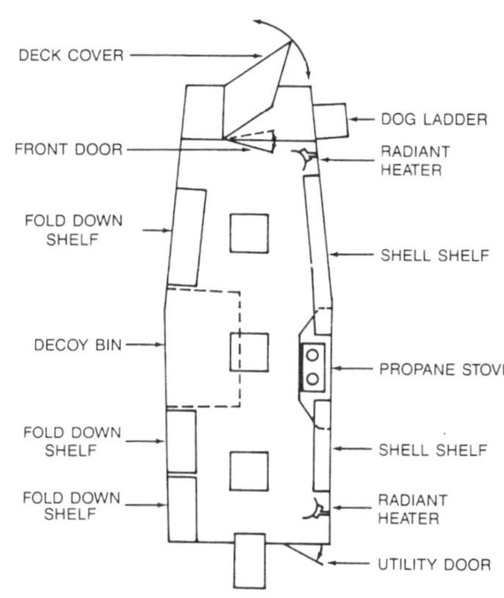

Figure 2. Boat Blind Floor plan

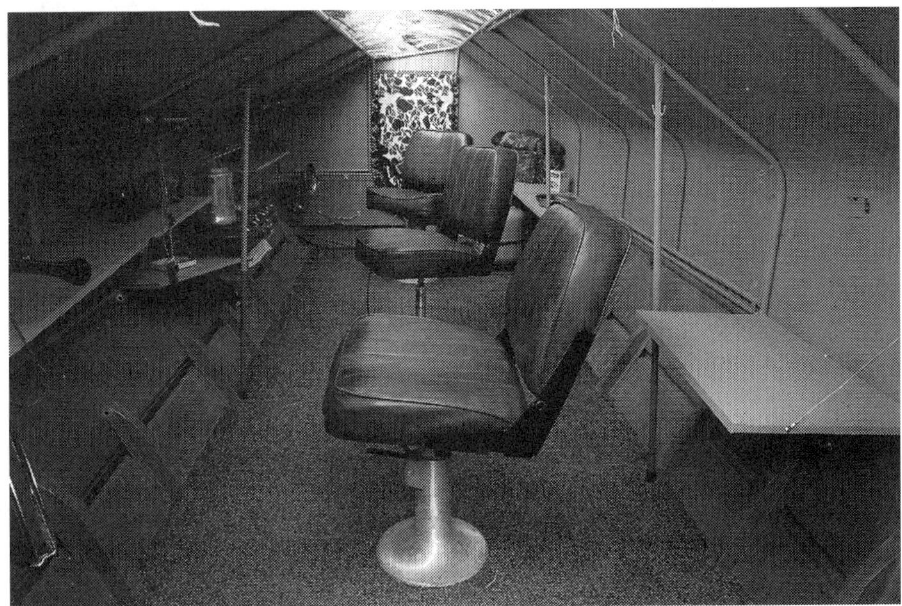

Ivan Mothershead
Charlotte, NC

PVC Johnboat Blind

An inexpensive, easy to build boat blind with adjustable frame height. Constructed on a 16 foot johnboat.

Construction Notes: Measure the length of the boat that you intend to frame, while allowing for vertical columns. This should give you a "ballpark" figure for the amount of conduit you will need to purchase. You may want to buy more pipe and fittings than you need; they can always be returned once you have completed the framework.

A rule of thumb is to purchase four times the length of your boat of 1-1/4 inch PVC, and five times the inside width. Each end of your boat will have two cross beams running across the bottom of the boat, and the center will have one.

You are basically building a box frame over your boat. The height of the blind can be adjusted with the (six) one inch diameter PVC posts, sliding them up or down in the 1-1/4 inch main posts. You will also be able to adjust the blind for shooting from either side because the top frame supports slide to either side of the boat by using 1-1/2 inch tee connectors to the one inch frame supports. On boats smaller than 16 feet, fewer cross beams are needed.

The vertical support length is determined during blind construction. Sitting in the boat in a hunting position will give you an idea on the height needed. You may consider keeping the blind height slightly lower than eye level.

The frame of the blind has another frame which slides up and down in the main framework. This allows you to adjust the blind to numerous positions. For this frame, use one inch PVC. You will need three cross bars the width of your boat. Cut two of them to make four separate cross bars, which will slide to either side of the boat.

Don't skimp on fittings. You will need four 1-1/2 inch (four-ways) for the center post, and sleeves to fit in them in order to bring them down to fit the 1-1/4 inch main frame. Approximately 30 (1-1/4 inch) tee fittings will be needed. Six "L" fittings are required for the inside frame to fit the one inch pipe.

Begin building the blind by cutting the PVC for your basic main frame. Initially you want to cut these longer than needed and lay them out in the boat. Trim to size as needed. Put the frame together with your fittings as you go along in construction. DO NOT USE ANY GLUE AT THIS POINT. Build the bottom frame, then decide on the desired height of your blind; now cut the vertical center posts and insert them. Cut short individual pieces to attach to the tee fittings. The PVC does not run through the fittings; each piece is separate. The center post is the only difficult post; it uses 1-1/2 inch (four-way) fittings reduced with 1-1/4 inch reducing fittings.

Next build the cross beams that attach to the vertical sliding posts. These will consist of three pieces of one inch PVC cut to the width of the boat, and then attached to the six pieces of one inch conduit; the height of the main posts. Cut the vertical pieces first, attach the "L" fittings, then cut the cross bars to fit. Before you attach the cross beams to the vertical supports, slip on (2) 1-1/4 inch tee fittings on each end cross bar and four on the center bar. These will attach to the 1-1/4 inch PVC cross bars which can now be cut to size.

After you attach the cross bars, check all your fittings. Make sure your vertical column slides up and down inside the main posts, and the cross bars slide from side to side with ease. This will be a welcome addition when it becomes cold and rainy.

Once you are satisfied that the blind is basically squared and solid, you can drill the holes for your support screws. The PVC will hold in most cases without the support screws or glue, but add durability during windy conditions. Support screws are inserted at each tee fitting. On the main posts you may want to add a wing nut. You may also want to glue the main vertical supports on the outside only. If you get glue on the inside, the vertical PVC will not slide up and down. Remember, the vertical posts are inside your main posts and will not slide if screws are added.

Rubber bungee cords or straps can be used to attach the blind to your boat. Paint the framework any color you desire. Acrylic enamel paints have a tendency to bond to PVC better than most other paints.

Daryl McConnell
Leo, IN

Fourteen Foot Frame with PVC Construction

Fourteen foot flat bottom boat with 57 inch top width and 36 inch bottom width. PVC (3/4 inch) frame blind.

Construction Notes: With a 1-1/4 inch gunwale rail around this particular boat, the tees will snap over the railing if cut slightly over center. The tee connector used is 1 x 1 x 3/4 inch, which enables use of 3/4 inch pipe for the cross members. For connections throughout the frame, use 3/4 x 3/4 x 3/4 inch "T"s with the back portion cut in half. These can be easily fastened with small sheet metal screws. The cross members can be cut to any length to give you the desired viewing height.

The connection of PVC pipe twists together to give a secure lock, therefore a permanent fixture is not required. This will also enable you to tear the whole framework apart while going to and from the hunting site. Complete assembly can be done from inside the boat.

The cover consists of two pieces of 48 inch camo burlap, seamed together in the center. Burlap is easy to sew on a home machine using standard threads. The cover has an elastic bottom that is made by looping the material on the bottom and feeding a long strand of bungee through the loop. Bungee can be found at most hardware stores. Flaps are cut on the top of the corner for gunny holes. Excess material may be added to oversize the flaps. Velcro straps are placed in the gunny holes to fasten the material over the frame. For longer life of the burlap cover, all cut edges should be turned under and sewn.

Material List:

Frame:

- (5) 10 foot by 3/4 inch PVC pipe
- (8) 1 x 1 x 3/4 inch tee connectors
- (10)3/4 x 3/4 x 3/4 inch tee connectors
- (1) box of sheet metal screws

Cover:

- (11) yards of burlap camo
- (2) foot-long strips of Velcro
- (30) foot-long stands of bungee cord

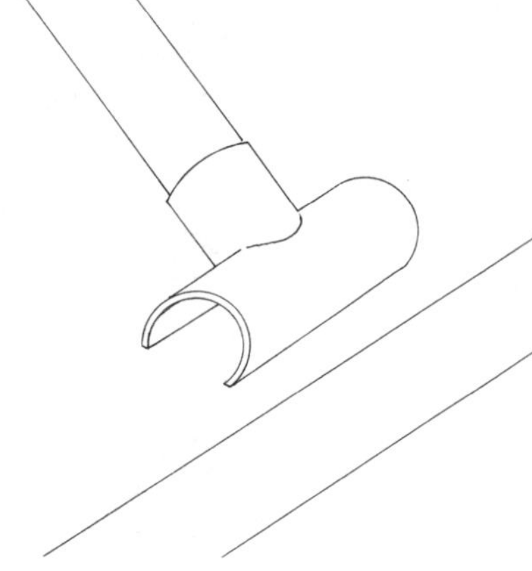

Mark Fincel
Columbia, MO

Large Boat with Half-Inch Conduit Frame Blind

This blind took into consideration full overhead cover, low profile, weathertight and lightweight construction materials, easy to mount on a boat, accommodates seven dozen decoys, providing comfortable accommodations for four adults.

Construction Notes: The boat used for this blind is an 1860 welded john manufactured by Generation III of Lebanon, MO. It has an 83 inch beam and is powered by a 40 horse Mercury with electric start, tiller handle, long shaft, and tilt/trim.

The blind frame is constructed of half inch conduit (IMC) and assembled completely by welding. Each member of the conduit frame is painted and wrapped with burlap to prevent rust and minimize the need for repainting.

The weathertight skin for the blind is a fabric consisting of a polyester base coated with Poly Vinyl Chloride (PVC). The fabric is 22 mil thick, weighs two pounds per square yard, cannot be torn by hand, and is difficult to puncture with a knife. The fabric is attached to the frame with drywall screws at the top member and at the bottom member, just above the gunwales. The fabric, as manufactured, has a flat black finish on one side. However, you may consider painting olive drab or other camo color.

Nylon netting is affixed to the frame, outside the skin, with polyethylene pipe (cut in half lengthwise) and screws. The netting is a #18 Nylon Seine with 1-1/2 x 3 inch openings, and allows the application of a variety of camouflages such as bulrush, rip gut, smart weed, or tree branches (e.g. cedar boughs). Bulrush was used in this case due to its ability to withstand highway driving as well as its ability to match well in the area hunted.

The overhead cover is constructed of steel conduit overlaid by standard chicken wire with a two inch mesh opening. Natural camo material is lightly woven into the chicken wire, allowing full visibility. The cover opens with the back following in garage door track and the front sliding on top of two shaped pieces of conduit. Additionally, the cover is spring-loaded with the use of pulleys and elastic cord to quickly open when desired.

Shelving, consisting of 1 x 12 pine, is provided for storing equipment, including decoys. The decoy storage shelving is affixed to conduit support members and is constructed to store one layer of duck or goose decoys per level.

The gas tank, two batteries, and propane tank can be stored on top of the floatation pods provided with the boat. Three automotive accessory lights illuminate the interior of the blind; spotlight and running light receptacles are wired into the reserve battery. Five transom light pole storage clips are fastened to the top member of the blind: the pliable rubber fingers of the clips hold 20, 12, and 10 gauge barrels firmly without marring the finish.

Material List:
310 feet 1/2 inch conduit (IMC)
27 sq. yards Polyester (PVC) fabric
(75 feet) 1 x 12 pine
5 pounds of #18 Nylon seine net
15 sq. yards burlap
60 feet 1-1/2 inch polyethylene pipe
16 feet garage door track
3 garage door wheels and brackets
Drywall screws, chicken wire, clips, lights

Pam & Troy Biddle
Terre Haute, IN

EMT (3/4 inch) Frame Blind on a 16' Boat

A johnboat blind on a 16 foot Alumacraft. The boat has no seats, includes an access opening for a retriever, supports three hunters and a dog, and is covered with a fabric called Twill (a medium weight, durable material).

Construction Notes: Foam insulation is placed in the bottom of the boat and bolted down with 3/4 inch plywood to the frame to make the bottom level. Indoor/ Outdoor carpet (dark grey or other acceptable color) is glued down to the plywood. Dark grey paint mixed with sand is brushed on the front and back upper decks. The sand gives the surface a non-slick finish. Holes are drilled on the right side of the boat in the front and back to install mounts for portable light poles. When the lights are not needed, they are kept in a Velcro carrier just behind the upper deck. The wiring is threaded down the right side from the front to the back (keeping) the wires hidden), running to a toggle switch box and then to the battery. All connections are soldered. Black heat shrink was put around the two wires (18 gauge) to hold them together and conceal them.

The blind frame, made out of 3/4 inch EMT conduit, is welded. It is lightweight and sits just inside the edge of the boat. The frame is sprayed a flat color to tone down the shiny conduit. The center of the boat frame is left open to allow occupants to walk freely from front to back. Seats consists of mounts with removable pedestals, one near the bow and one on the back deck. A five gallon pail is used as a seat for a third hunter.

The fabric blind is sewn to cover the three openings at the top of the blind so it could be pulled closed on rainy days or rolled back to one side and secured with Velcro straps on clear days.

The entire cover, once sewn together, is sprayed with two cans of 3M Scotchguard. After it dries, the cover is painted with the same color the boat is painted. Marsh Grass material is sewed to the base of the blind cover, allowing it to move slightly in the wind. Elastic is put at the bottom of the cover around the front and the back so it could be pulled down over the frame of the boat and then secured with nylon straps to the carrying handles of the boat. There are two straps each in the front and back that hook and unhook very easily with plastic latches.

The cover is rolled up on one side of the frame and secured by bungee cords when transporting the rig. A chain, similar to a log chain, but not as heavy, is inserted inside the overlapped material at the bottom of both sides of the blind. This makes the material stay in place and the chain is secured at both ends in the front and back so that it cannot slide from one side to the other.

Elastic with Velcro sewn together is attached so that the top of the cover could be fastened to the boat frame without much effort. They are placed on the inside of the boat to make the cover fit securely.

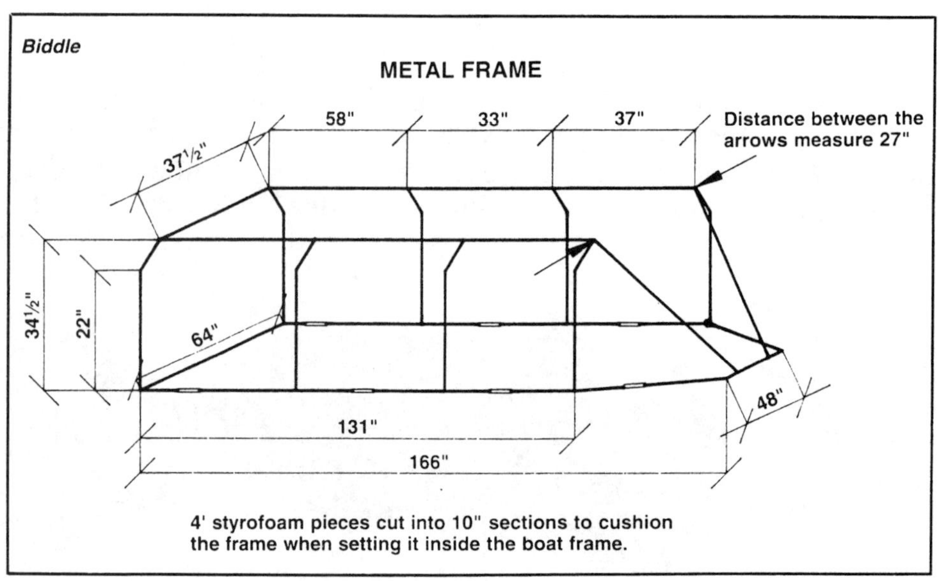
Biddle
METAL FRAME
58"
33"
37"
Distance between the arrows measure 27"
37½"
34½"
22"
64"
48"
131"
166"
4' styrofoam pieces cut into 10" sections to cushion the frame when setting it inside the boat frame.

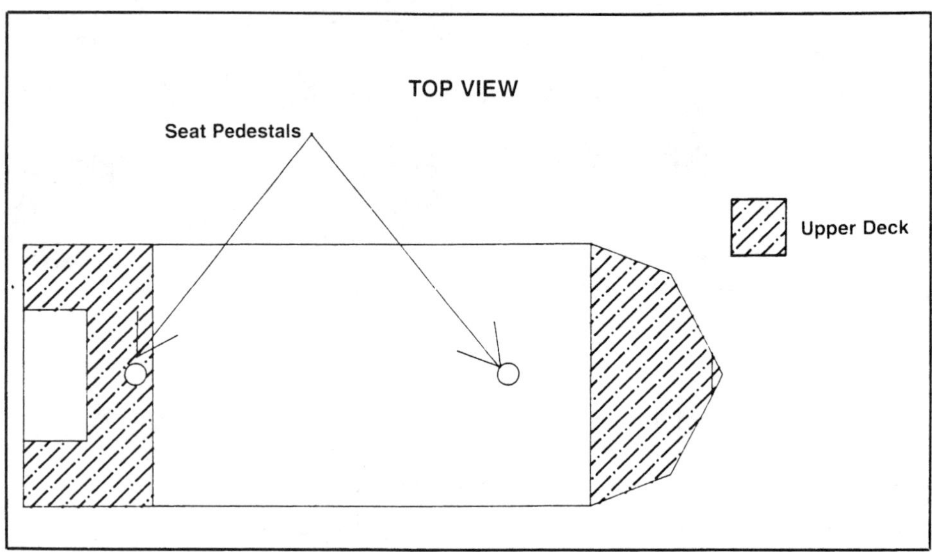
TOP VIEW
Seat Pedestals
Upper Deck

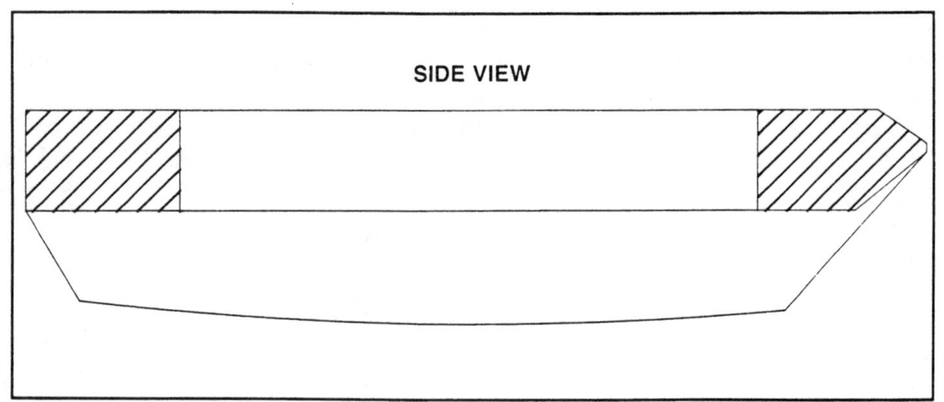
SIDE VIEW

Peter Pattee
Ames, IA

Small Frame Blind (Oak Spreader)

An inexpensive blind for small (10-14 foot) duck boats that allows easy raising and lowering of blind for retrieves if you are without a retriever.

Construction Notes: The basic principal is that two lines run from the bow through the oak bow spreader (placed and tied to be comfortably behind the hunter who faces aft when raised) with enough remaining to tie onto the stern spreader. Two lines also run from the stern corners to the stern spreader and are tied to be sufficiently far from the hunter's front to allow gun handling, freedom of movement, dog disciplining, etc. The spreaders have two (1 inch) holes near each end: the inner holes accept the upper ends of the supports, while the outer holes provide tie-points for the lines. Final stability in the upright position is gained by drawing the ends of the lines leading from the bow spreader tight and tying them to the stern spreader. Attached near the rail of the hull from bow to stern are several eye-bolts (12-16 inches apart) to which is attached nylon or similar netting which, when properly adjusted, adds considerable rigidity to the erected blind.

The aluminum supports that hold the spreaders upright can be made so that their length is adjustable, although experience has shown that once a proper length is identified--which depends on seat height, stature of the shooter, and personal preference--a single length is sufficient for all four supports.

For the aluminum johnboats, the supports consist of a length of aluminum tubing (3/4 inch diameter electrical conduit). A two-inch length of continuously threaded stock (1/4 inch-3/8 inch diameter) passes through the tubing about two inches from one end and is held with nuts on either side serving to support the spreader. The lower end accepts the shaft of a laboratory clamp whose fingers are allowed to fully open (Note: the threaded adjustment screws for the clamps are discarded) and they simply fit loosely over the rail of the hull. Hulls longer than approximately 10 feet might benefit from an additional spreader and extra supports.

When collapsed by pulling out the supports, the netting falls into the hull. For sneaking up on a sitting bird when the wind is light, oars are easily slipped through the enlarged openings of the netting. The covering on the netting can be natural vegetation (with or without sewn burlap or canvas on the inner face of the net to better hide movement and help cut any wind), or the military style netting with camouflage attached. If hunting with a dog, leave the opening across the stern free of permanent netting, but perhaps with a flap or extra section that can be added when needed.

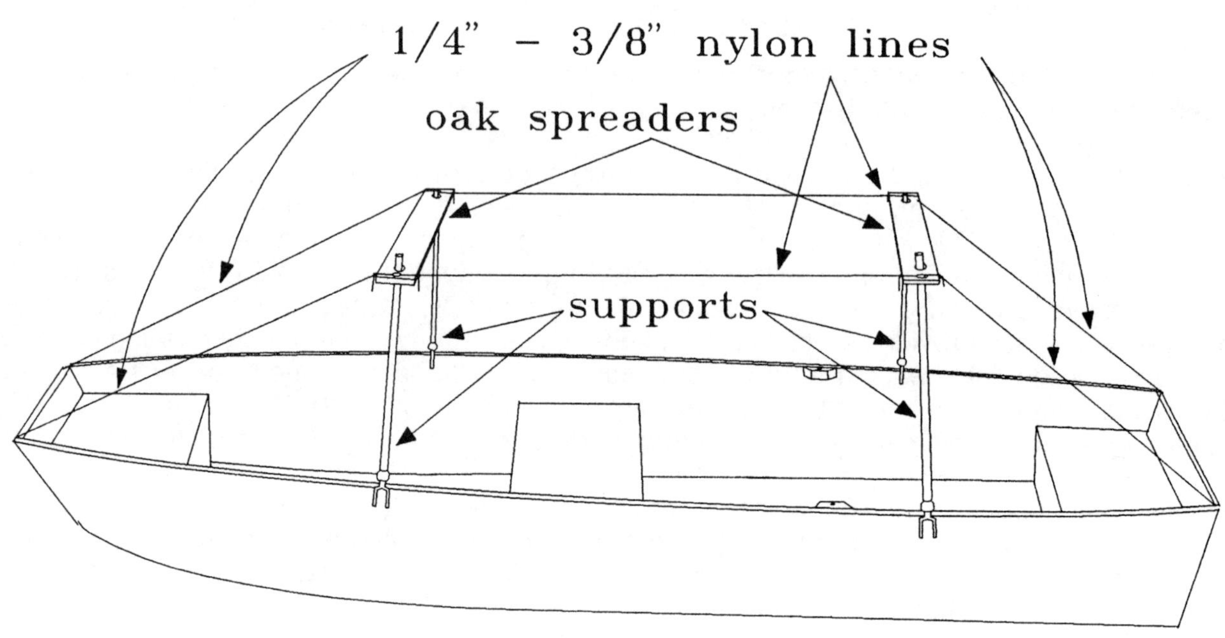
1/4" - 3/8" nylon lines
oak spreaders
supports

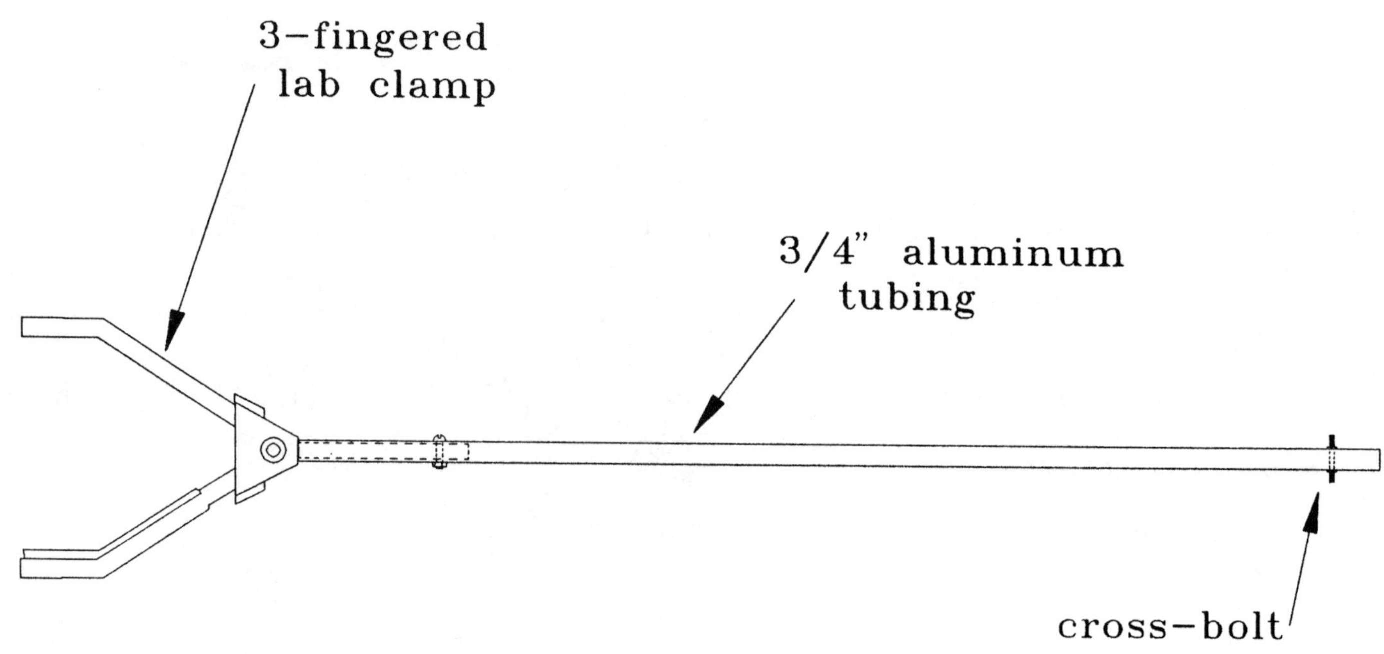
3-fingered
lab clamp
3/4" aluminum
tubing
cross-bolt

C.W. James
Omaha, NE

Boat Blind on 16 Foot Boat

This 72" wide Polar Kraft initially had only one seat which is at the stern end of the boat. This made the initial task of construction easier since the majority of the inside of the boat was open.

Start by constructing two stern-to-bow bunks, one for seating, the other for stowing upwards of 72 magnum decoys. The bunk framing consists of wood 1 x 2's using a header and a base and studs in the middle, similar to a stud wall.

The floor is cut from 3/8" exterior plywood. This is riveted to ribs of the boat's floor. Cut the width so that it will not cover the entire floor of the boat under the seats and bunks. Leave the floor exposed in these areas so that water draining from the decoys runs to the rear of the boat. The walkway (space between the seats and bunks) is left at 18" (the same size as the top opening of the blind).

The top of the seats and bunks are built of 1/2" exterior plywood for more strength and are hinged to open from the front. This allows for enough space behind the hinges so that when opened, the doors will lay back against the sides of the blind and not straight up and down, where they would always be slamming shut. The seating area consists of two 4 foot doors and one that is 2 feet. This allows for easier access to the storage space below without everyone needing to move. Front steering is a must in this type of rig as you must be "up front" to have the visibility needed to operate the boat safely.

Much time is spent "form-fitting" the seats and bunk tops to the taper of the boat as it narrows towards the front. The width lost to the taper is taken from the space behind the hinges, thus allowing for the doors to remain as big as possible.

Another decision to make is whether to build a "high-low" blind or one equal in height in both the front and rear of the blind. Comfort in extreme weather and the ability to properly conceal one's body leads to the the "high-low" type of construction. Sitting on the seats with a hat on, measure the distance from the floor to the top of the hat. In this case the "high-side" turned out to be 4 feet above the floor. The front, or "low-side," of the blind is built at eye level to the seated hunters. This turns out to be 8 inches lower than the "high-side."

The length of the blind is 14' from the stern to the front door. Since the Polar Kraft has a 3' deck on the front of the boat, the blind is extended on to the deck about one foot. This extra foot is utilized for the construction of a storage bin on the "high-side" and left open on the "low-side" for a place for your dog.

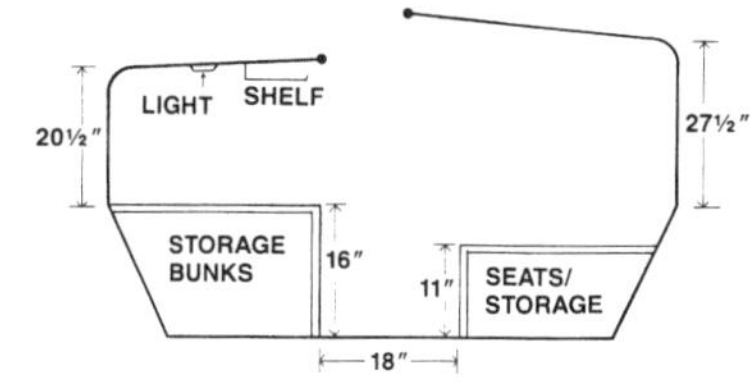

The blind framing is constructed from 3/4" electrical conduit with the exception of the ribs that attach the base to the header which are half-inch diameter conduit.

The 3/4" base is bolted through the gunnel and allowed to follow the natural taper of the boat. This meant that as the ribs were cut and welded they decreased in size, both vertical and width, as you moved to the front of the boat. The ribs are placed at 12" centers. When completed, the 3/4" inside headers are covered with rubber pipe insulation for comfort as well as safety. Guns leaning against bare metal headers may slide and fall. This way they stay put.

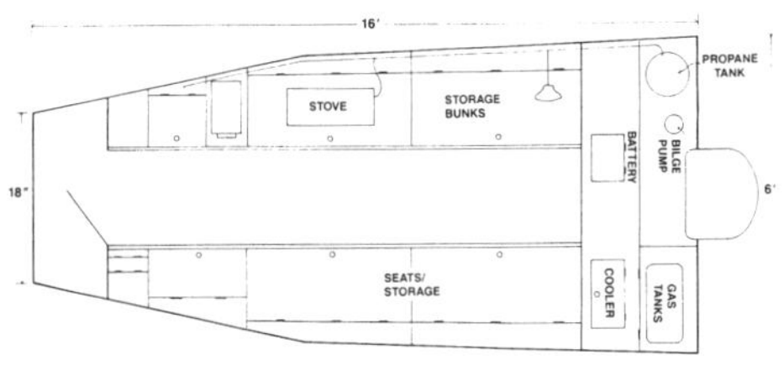

The two ends of the blind are constructed out of 3/8" plywood because of the strength it provided. The door is likewise cut to fit the "high-low" angle and was made from plywood. Extend the blind over the rear 28" of the boat to completely cover the rear area of the boat and allow for someone to lay on the factory installed rear seat to take a nap and be totally covered from weather. This covers the motor area, gas cans, radios, propane tank and battery storage area.

After cutting, binding and welding all the ribs and after installing the front and rear ends, the actual "skinning" of the blind is next. Use .032 aluminum sheeting purchased in 3' x 8' sheets. The aluminum is pop riveted to the 1/2" ribs and extended down and riveted to the gunnel, thus making the blind permanently attached to the boat. Some "form-fitting" of the aluminum had to be done to allow for the taper of the boat. The seams are over-lapped and glued, using a special metal adhesive. Don't spare the rivets.

After the blind is "skinned," a 2" x 4" wire mesh is attached to the outside of the blind to provide the addition of whatever covering you choose to use. The wire mesh is attached to lengths of 1/2" conduit and bolted through the 1/2" ribs of the blind. This allows for the mesh to be removed in order to clean or change the covering as hunting conditions warrant.

Center steering and controls are added to the boat along with a complete electrical system allowing for running lights, horn, bilge pump, seven interior lights, AM/FM stereo and CB radio. The boat is equipped with two batteries, one battery for all the electrical items and one strictly for starting purposes. A propane stove and 12,000 BTU heater also are included and run off of a standard 20 lb. propane tank mounted in the rear of the boat. The propane and two six-gallon tanks are all located in the rear of the boat and away from any heat sources as well as guns and hunters. The propane hose also has an outlet for an additional appliance in the front of the boat. The boat is powered by a 40 hp OMC outboard.

The interior of the blind is painted and waterproofed with a "water sealer." In order to save space the battery is set in the rear seat in a separate compartment. A small cooler is built into the rear seat for storage of food and drinks. Another compartment is built in the front of the boat for the storage of pots, pans and other cooking utensils. The walkway and sides of the bunks and seats are carpeted with marine carpeting for ease of cleaning, and the seven interior lights provide all the light needed for pre-dawn setting up and at night, or if used as a camper.

For traveling and at night, the blind can be totally "buttoned up" by using a 26" x 14" piece of vinyl roofing material that has 3/8" grommets along both sides. This cover is attached using rubber cords. Smaller pieces of covering material (26" x 3') are also tossed in the boat when there is less than a "full house," so that if the weather is a factor you can close off unused sections of the blind.

Canary Reed Grass was cut from road ditches the previous fall and used as a camo covering. It proved to be an excellent cover and withstood the many miles of highway travel. For the top opening a "plastic broom straw" is used, although you may need to substitute with a different cover since it is difficult to locate this product. The straw covering is anchored under the 1/2" length of conduit that holds the top end of the wire mesh to the boat. The plastic broom straw is very tough and will withstand much abuse without breaking and is not affected by the weather.

~ 4 ~
Open Water Rigs

John Videmschek
St. Louis, MO
Dennis Juengling
Robert Jenne
Charles Milano

Floating Island

An 8 x 12 foot stationary floating island, with 55 gallon drums used for floatation. Used in a somewhat protected open water area, not subject to large wave action. This particular blind is used on the Mississippi River, near Elsberry, Missouri.

Construction Notes: Floor: The floor consists of (6) 2 x 10 inch x 12 foot and (2) 2 x 10 inch x 8 foot wolmanized lumber. The 12 foot boards are placed on 22 inch centers. The diameter of the 55 gallon drums is 22 inches. By placing the 12 foot boards on 22 inch centers, it allows for the top portion of the barrels to be cradled between the framework. In addition, this spacing keeps the barrels about 2 inches below the 3/4 inch plywood flooring. To allow for the gap in the center, nail (2) 12 foot (2 x 10's) together with cripples. As a result, there will be four barrels in each line, for a total of 16 barrels. The barrels are next bound to the framework by using nylon bailing, the type used in packaging of boxes. Construct this framework on a boat trailer and attach the barrels to the framework while on the trailer. Then back the trailer down a boat ramp, push one end of the deck into the water, and then push the other end up into the air and over, to allow it to fall on the barrels. The deck, made of 3/4 inch CDX plywood, is then nailed onto the frame. Both sides of the deck on this particular rig were previously treated with driveway sealer. In each of the four corners, 1/2 inch metal 90 degree corner braces are bolted in place, using (4) 4 inch long 1/2 inch bolts.

Walls: All of the walls are constructed out of construction grade 2 x4's, and are four feet high. The framework is laid out on 16 inch centers. The front wall is 12 feet long. The two side walls are 7 feet 9 inches long. The back of the blind consists of a four foot center opening to allow entry, and has two small 3 foot 9 inch long back walls. Corrugated tin is then nailed to the wall framework. Tin is used instead of plywood to help withstand the weather better, and to minimize weight. Next the walls are painted inside and out with a driveway sealer. A shooting shelf is constructed approximately 12 inches below the top of the front wall. A series of cripples nailed between the framework to allow for setting shells, calls, thermos, or other necessary items.

Outriggers: The purpose of the outriggers is to allow for shrubbing the blind in a pancake effect. The outriggers are constructed out of construction grade 2 x 4's, in a truss-like manner. Four outriggers on the front wall, and three on each of the side walls. The outriggers are nailed to the top of each wall and hung on a joist hanger attached to the 2 x 10 deck framework. Pieces of 1 x 4 inch wood are nailed across the outriggers to facilitate tacking of the shrubbing.

Boat blind Outriggers: The purpose of this outrigger is to facilitate having the boat next to the blind, and to continue the pancake shrubbing effect. The outrigging is constructed out of 2 x 4's in a roof, truss-like fashion. A total of six trusses are needed for the boat blind to allow for proper concealment of a 20 foot boat. The top of the truss is nailed to the top of the back wall, and the bottom of the truss is hung on a joist hanger. In order to make these connections, four (8 foot 2 x 4's) are nailed to the framework of the back walls. Once again, these outriggers are interconnected with 1 x 4's. After putting the boat blind outriggers in place, some additional stability will be needed at the ends. This can be done by adding additional 2 x 4's on the under side of the truss, and construct a cradle for three additional barrels. This will help eliminate some of the tension on those trusses and increase the stability of the blind overall. The barrels are wired in place.

Roof: The roof is constructed using 2 x 4 inch framework with tin as the covering material. It is twelve feet long by four feet wide. A slight pitch is given to the roof by nailing angled cripples at both ends of the roof. It is further supported in the middle by two upright braces running from the floor deck to the roof framework. The open shooting area towards the front wall is partitioned off the make four shooting stalls. This is accomplished by angle cutting a 2 x 4 and nailing it in place between the roof and the top of the front wall. Shooting hole coverings are fashioned out of willows into a square to cover any of the holes that might not be in use when hunting.

Anchors and Cables: Anchors are made of 1/2 x 5 inch pieces of steel angle. Using a fork design (two prongs approximately 20 inches each) welded to a piece of similar steel approximately 24 inches long, a piece of 2 inch thick wall pipe (24 inches long), is welded at an angle of approximately 60 degrees. To complete the anchor assembly, a 1/4 inch steel cable is attached to both the anchor and the angle bolted to the exterior floor joist using two cable clamps on each end. A total of five anchors are made. The four corner anchor cables are each approximately 30 feet long. The center (up river) cable is approximately 60 feet long.

Anchors & Cable:
*Various lengths of (1/2 x 5 inch) metal angle
*(5) pieces of thick wall (2 inch) galvanized pipe, each 24 inches long
*(4) pieces of 1/4 inch metal cable, each approximately 30 feet long, and one piece of 1/4 inch cable approximately 60 feet long.
*(10) 1/4 inch cable camps
*Numerous 2 x 4s & 1 x 4s (8 & 12 foot lengths)
*Galvanized corrugated sheet metal (cut to length)
*Galvanized nails (6s, 8s, 16s, & roofing)
*10 gallons of driveway sealer
*(9) 1/2 inch metal angles
*(14) metal 2 x 4 joist hangers
*Nylon banding material (1 inch wide) & clips
*Galvanized wire

Jan Nordin
Alma, AR

Floating Island

Complete with dog ramp. Used in relatively protected open water areas.

Construction Notes:

*Blind has double bottom with epoxy on all four sides of bottom.
*All seams and bottom are covered with fiberglass cloth.
*All joints are mitered or lapped.
*Sides and boat well are covered with seine material with grass sewn on.
*Material is secured to blind with cup hooks.
*To transport to or from water, wing nuts are removed from the five struts, removable screws are removed from steel arms, netting disconnected from side struts and boat well is rolled in against blind. Approximately five minutes required for procedure.
*Dog ladder removes from slots for transportation.
*Blind may be anchored by pipes driven into the bottom or by cables attached to weights.

Material List:

*Approximately 12 sheets A-C plywood (1/2 inch)
*Approximately 234 feet of 2 x 4
*Two 4 foot 4 x 4s
*Two 5 foot 4 x 4s
*Six gallons epoxy resin
*Fiberglass cloth
*1 1/2-inch screws
*Two l x 4 steel tubing (12 ft.)
*Six dozen cup hooks
*100 feet minnow seine material
*1 1/2 4 x 8 styrofoam blocks (17")
*Approximately 70 feet of 2 x 2s
*Assorted hinges, wing nuts, corner braces, etc.

SIDE VIEW

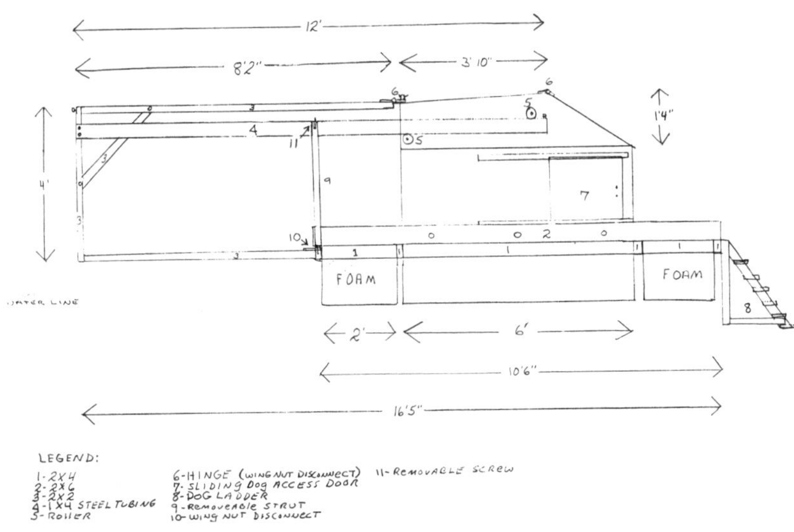

FRONT VIEW

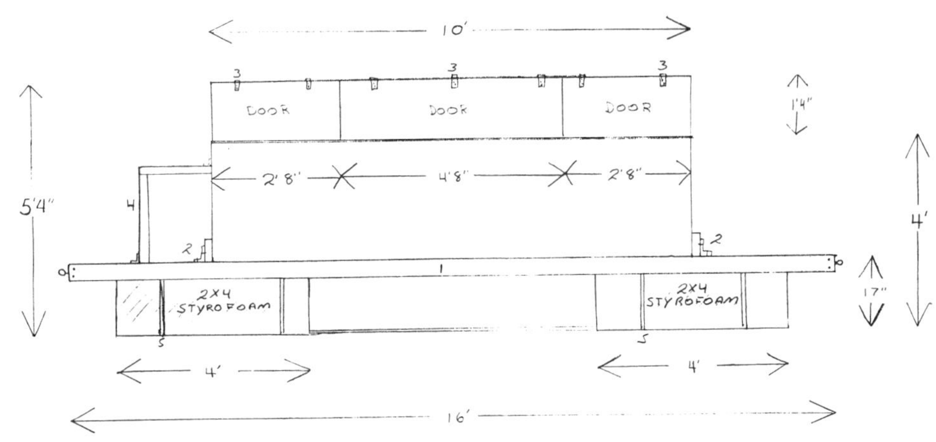

LEGEND

1-2X4
2-2X6
3-HINGES
4-DOG ENTRY FRAME (2X2)
5-NYLON RETAINER STRAPS

Pontoons

One spring while I was on my way to the popular Fish Point State Game Area at the eastern edge of Michigan's Saginaw Bay, I noticed a "For Sale" sign on a pontoon boat in a farmer's yard. Price: $1500. It didn't take long for me to throw my Ford pickup in reverse in order to take a look at what could have been the last straw in a reasonably stable marriage during that period of time.

During the warmer months, pontoons can be seen on most any inland lake across the United States. They are, for the money, one of the most inexpensive and versatile fishing or cruising boats around. They are used for everything from sea-going parties to casting plugs in the shallows for bass.

This versatility has led duck hunters to adapt these units into personalized duck hunting boats. But the concept is not new and has been around for several decades.

Back in the 1940's and '50's, bigwater hunters would use large, extremely heavy cedar logs as flotation devices. Two of these giant logs would be the basis for a floating blind, usually anchored in a "hot spot" out in the deep water. Unlike today's lightweight pontoons, these wooden predecessors were constructed in such a way as to provide a floating shelter for a smaller duck boat. The hunters would build these units to allow for a transport boat to motor into the center of the floating blind. Adequate decking would be provided on the blind for hunters to sit in relative comfort, waiting for the flight ducks to come winging down into the decoys.

The nature of these cedar log blinds prevented the hunters from moving them to different locations each day; instead, they were towed to a predetermined spot at the beginning of the season and would then be moved only if absolutely necessary.

In contrast, today's pontoons are lightweight and can be outfitted with a motor and used as both a blind and transport unit for hunters, dogs, and gear. Some of the pontoons are filled with urethane foam which makes them buoyant enough to float a Sherman tank. However, it is also an added cost, since it can run you several hundred dollars to have foam injected into a pair of pontoons. If you plan to purchase a used pontoon, check to see if the pontoons are urethane-filled or if a similar flotation material has been used. It's an added feature, but not absolutely necessary. Pontoons that are not urethane-filled will need to be checked from time to time to make sure there are no leaks or potential areas that are prone to leak.

Most waterfowlers, when looking for used pontoons, seek out the basic necessities: two reasonably solid pontoons and a good frame. For big water use, the frame can be a critical item. Some pontoon manufacturers use an "S" frame that is tack-welded to the pontoons. This may be fine for cruising around a

small lake, but for serious hunting on big water and in bad weather, it can cause problems. So be sure the undercarriage is strong; usually those units that are held together with channel iron are the strongest.

Another consideration is the deck. A "treated" deck means different things to different companies. The type you will want is a pressure treated deck so that it will survive more than a couple of seasons without rotting.

A final note when shopping around. Look for 22" tubes on the larger boats, they will handle the water much better and will provide a greater degree of safety.

With this in mind, the rest is a matter of personal design. Do you plan on hunting with more than three or four people in your blind? Since sizes range from approximately 14 to 25 feet, you will need to determine how much time, effort, and material you wish to put into your outfit. It's no different than building a house: the more square footage, the more it costs to build.

Size, however, will not have a major effect on maneuverability of the rig. Many pontoons handle quite well, even in somewhat rough water, but the biggest problem is with the craft "nose-diving" into a wave when too much weight is put forward such as when your overweight retriever takes a stroll to the bow. From the owners of pontoons that I have talked to, this does not seem to be a major concern since the boat manages to bounce back without too much difficulty. Let's hope your dog does.

The only other slight drawback is that pontoons have never been likened to offshore cigarette race boats. In other words, speed is not one of their greatest assets. Many pontoons have outboards ranging from 25 to 60 horse power which, depending on the size of the boat, will get you where you're going, but certainly not at any record speeds. Then again, I know of very few duck boats that are set up for water skiing.

One of the advantages of using a pontoon for waterfowling is the room and comfort they provide for the gunners. A 14-foot pontoon provides ample room for three hunters, a dog and other gear. Decoys are strapped to the bow allowing for easy placement of the blocks as well as for picking up at day's end.

The materials used for construction of your duck boat can range from simple fiberboard to pressure treated wood. The problem with fiberboard is that it requires more work in the long run. It is not uncommon to need to replace it every three or four years.

Pressure treated wood may cost more, but will outlast conventional treated surfaces many times over. Personally, I'd rather spend time hunting than I would rebuilding my boat every few years.

The above deck design is a matter of personal taste and comfort. You can design it with just the basic camo side walls, a couple of gunning ports, and milk crates for seats, or go to a more elaborate design with dog ports, padded swivel captain chairs, gun racks, folding doors, food compartments, beverage coolers, and whatever else that may suit your needs.

For the basic unit however, I suggest a bench-type seat with some sort of back support. Each gunner should have his/her own shooting port cut out of the top of the boat, and consideration should be given to your retriever's needs. The bow may be the best place for a dog blind. It provides for easy view of the birds and also allows for effortless on and off. It keeps the wet dog away from you as well.

I have noticed a couple of pontoon boats that incorporated the use of a metal or wood frame that is used to support a canvas cover. This method of providing both camouflage and wind break would seem to work well. Any canvas shop, such as a tent and awning store, would more than likely be able to custom-fit a heavy duty canvas cover for your particular design. An option could include an all-weather cover complete with plastic windows for foul weather conditions. In addition, brown or dark green canvas is available in most canvas shops, making a natural camouflaging

color. Finishing touches would be to add natural vegetation to break up the boat's outline.

Whatever size pontoon you choose, bow and stern anchors are a must to keep the craft from swaying back and forth. Otherwise, you are liable to drift into your decoys.

Camouflaging a pontoon begins with the tubes and other metal parts. These must be properly prepared before the first coat of paint is brushed or sprayed. Next, the bright orange or blue indoor/outdoor carpet that is most generally found on pontoon decks must be spray painted with an appropriate camo color. If you buy a used boat, it will pay to first check the decking to make sure the flooring is solid and not in a deteriorating condition; if it shows severe wear, now is the time to replace it with new, treated wood.

The type of above-deck camouflaging you use will depend on the area you plan on hunting. For open water hunting in the northern states, cedar boughs are ideal, making your rig look like a small island to the birds. Place your decoys on the lee side of the "island."

For marsh use, cattails or burlap works quite well. Cattails can be woven into a wire mesh and wrapped around the boat. In either case, some natural vegetation should be used to break up the outline of the boat.

An option to motoring your pontoon to and from your particular hunting spot is to use a transport boat and then build your rig in such a way that you have a blind for the hunters and the transport boat. You design it so that you can tow it to a hunting location, anchor it, and then drive your transport boat into the center of the pontoon, just like they did in the '40s and '50s.

The idea is to have a maneuverable blind at a set location that can hide your fishing boat or runabout. If you travel several miles across water to your favorite hunting location, the use of a faster boat will permit easier transportation to and from the blind. The pontoon would still be designed as a shooting platform, using all the gimmicks needed to provide a reasonable amount of comfort, but would not be used for transportation.

If you plan on moving your pontoon overland from one location to another, you will obviously need some sort of trailer. Trailers are a matter of personal need and desires, at least in the case of pontoons, because if you only need a trailer to haul your pontoon to and from your hunting waters once a year, a used, inexpensive trailer may be all you need.

However, if you like to move from one body of water to another and require extensive travel, you would be well-advised to check your trailer out carefully. Pontoons do have special trailers and, like most anything, there are good trailers and not-so good trailers. But, as mentioned above, the money should be spent in proportion to the amount of use it will receive. Nuff said.

Any way you look at them, pontoons, whether simple or elaborate, add up to not only a practical waterfowl hunting boat, but can be an enjoyable off-season project that tests your design abilities as well as your construction skills.

Larry Longren
Newton, IA

Wood Blind on Johnboat

Used mostly in open water conditions, however could be used in marsh setting.

Construction Notes: If you're looking for a top notch rig, and don't mind putting in 300 man-hours into design and construction, consider this waterfowl boat.

The boat used for the blind is a sixteen foot Polar Craft flat-bottom john boat. The blind is permanently fixed to the gunnel by installing a one inch angle iron around the gunnel and affixing the up-right to the angle iron.

The first step is to construct a conduit frame, consisting of half-inch steel, except for the two fourteen foot center pieces which are 3/4 inch conduit. Next is the construction of the seats, bunks and lower storage on both sides of the boat. Small angle iron and half-inch conduit is used for the framework and 3/8 inch plywood is used for the bunk and storage doors.

The next step is to install the mechanical steering that is placed near the front for better viewing when running the boat. Follow this with the throttle, shift controls, shelving, radio, and other items you feel may be necessary around the counsel area. Also installed on this rig is a 20 lb. LP tank connnected to two 11,000 BTU heaters with quick connectors for easy hook-up and removal.

Twelve volt wiring is installed for interior and exterior running lights. There are six interior and shelf lights and the regulation running front and rear lights with a 350,000 candlepower front running light.

A front deck is placed on the remaining front two feet of the boat by using 3/4 inch plywood reinforced underneath with half-inch angle iron for supports.

Following this is the outer aluminum skin consisting of .020 aluminum, fastened with metal screws to the conduit framework. Woven wire fencing is fastened to the outer skin for stuffing with natural camo.

A door system that provides easy access while hunting and yet be as water tight as possible is the next consideration. Aluminum road signs purchased at a local junk yard are used for this portion of construction. The doors are overlapped with a piece of rubber, cut from old inner tubes to lap over for maximum water tightness.

The boat is powered by a 50 HP outboard with power tilt and trim and a stainless power prop. It will sleep three, is equipped with a two burner stove, two 12 volt plug-ins for TV and a second high-power light. Storage space for cooking pans, dishes, life jackets, waders, gas tank, and approximately 100 decoys completes this magnificent duck boat.

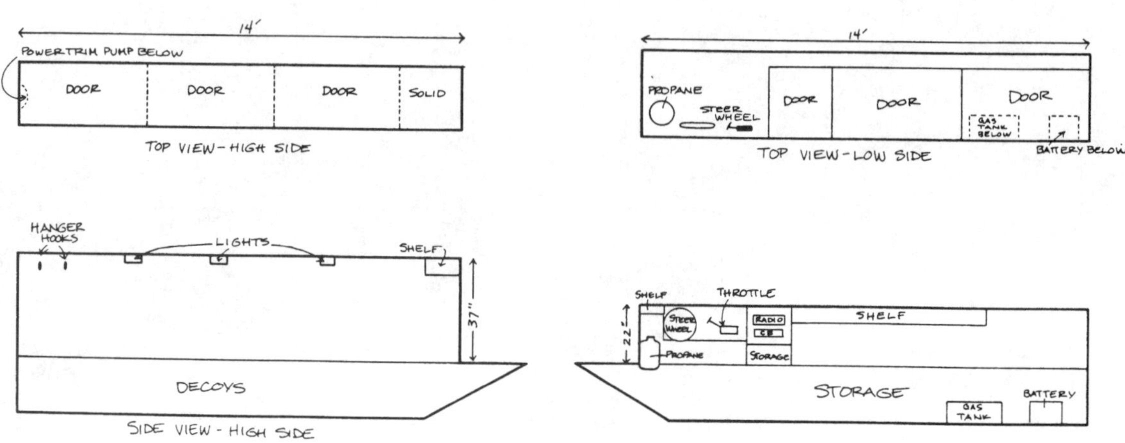

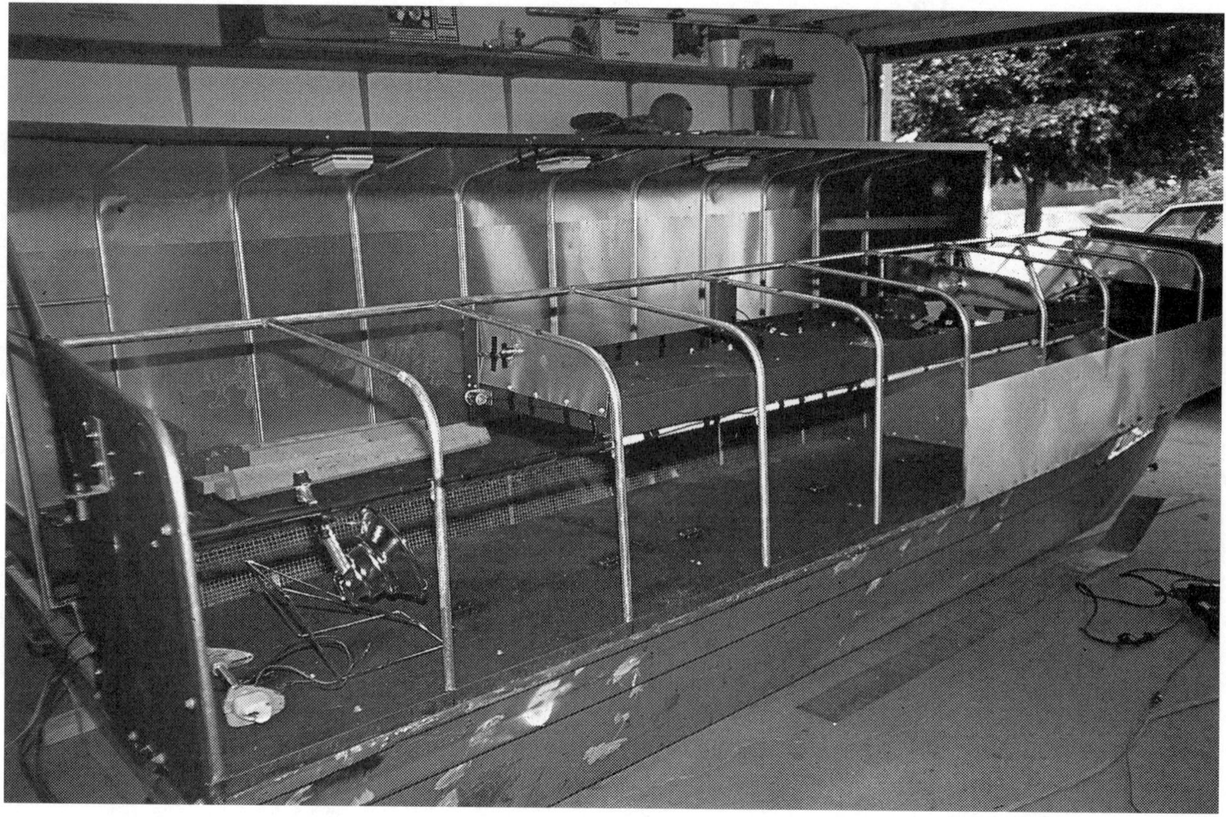

Brad Bachelder
Grand Rapids, MI

S.S. Merimack: Pontoon Blind

A 16 foot, twin pontoon, hunting platform. Marsh or open water use.

Construction Notes: This twin pontoon hunting rig is framed with welded steel, rustproofed with heavy gauge treated aluminum decking. The gunner compartment is a projectionless frame, with galvanized steel skin. The interior is spray insulated, has indoor/outdoor carpet, three gunning ports, three high-back swivel stools, and dual propane heaters. The pontoons are urethane foam filled for floatation safety.

The dimension of each pontoon is 16 feet; hunting box is 12 feet long, 5 feet wide, and 4 feet high. The port openings are 2 x 2 feet. The port covers have dual bolt locks. The hatch cover at the bow is 3 x 4 feet, is water tight, and is operated by dual hydraulic arms with a 45 degree opening radius.

The tender boat engages in a full length roller track at the bow, between the pontoons, concealing all but the motor under the blind. The roller track and hatch allow for rapid access to the tender boat, greatly reducing the number of cripples.

A very shallow draft allow this rig to work along the shoreline. Mud anchors consist of poles or four anchors. Camo is three tone flat marsh colors accented with black brush patterns overspray. L-shaped tabs are welded every two feet on the skin of the gunners compartment. The tabs are drilled and strung with nylon decoy cord, allowing attachment of cattail or other natural vegetation.

Larry Sack
North Platte, NE

Floating Boat Blind

Blind can be mounted on boat, or towed to hunting site. Used primarily in open water areas.

Construction Notes: This rig is set up for three hunters with three fully cushioned bench seats and a small bow seat. Two compartments in the rear of the boat (one on each side) are used for storage of life jackets, tool kit, binoculars, flashlights, extra gloves, etc.

The blind frame is made entirely of one inch square tubing. All joints are welded. The pontoons are 10 inch aluminum pipe 16 feet long. The frame is covered with chicken wire and overlapped with canvas for weather protection. Weeds are wired in small bundles and attached to the blind. Entering the blind is from the stern through two doors. The blind is 18 feet long, allowing for the entire boat and motor to be concealed. The boat is locked in with the use of boomers pulling the boat forward and up into the blind. The top is covered with three sets of lids which are covered with camo mesh so you can see out. There are eyebolts welded on the front and each side to attach anchor ropes. The blind floats extremely well when the boat exits to pick up birds, adjust decoys, etc. Although the hunters usually travel from the launch site to the hunting location with the boat in the blind, the blind can also be towed. The boat is much more stable in rough water when locked into the blind.

Although this rig is used mostly in open water, it does blend well with shoreline vegetation.

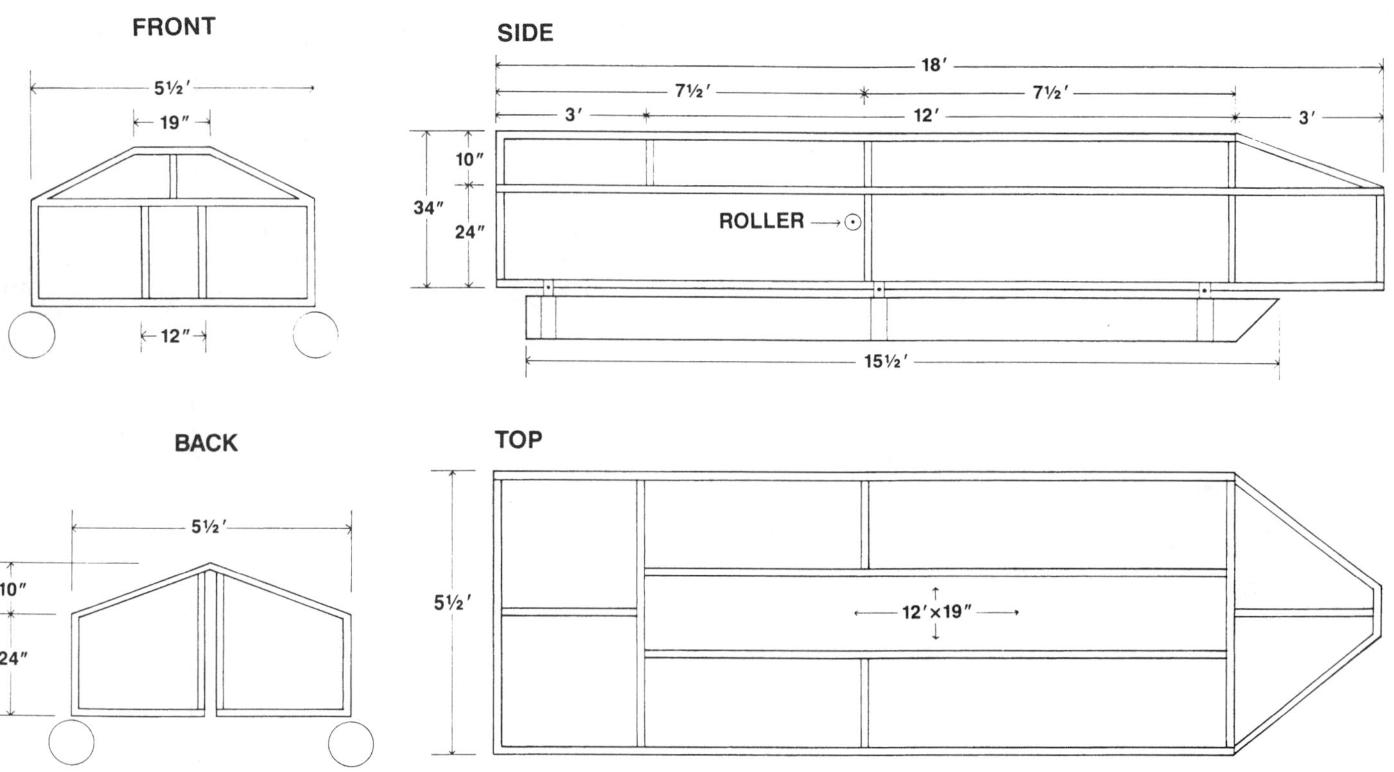

John Bendzsa
Terre Haute, IN

Elaborate Open Water Boat Blind

Canvas over aluminum frame blind mounted on a 17 foot commercial fishing boat. Used in open water hunting.

Construction Notes: The sides of this blind are framed using 1/4 x 2 inch wide cold rolled aluminum welded to the side of the boat, as well as attached to the wood inside the boat. The exterior is covered with 1/4 x 4 inch x 8 foot sheets of plywood; scored so it would bend and conform to the aluminum braces.

The aluminum braces are fastened to the seating area. Except for the half-inch thick plywood walkway down the center of the boat, all plywood used is 1/4 inch thick, keeping the overall weight to a minimum. The plywood center walkway is laid on the boat braces so that it minimizes contact with any water that may exist on the bottom of the boat. Several 3/8 inch holes are drilled in the plywood to allow water to flow to the bottom of the boat.

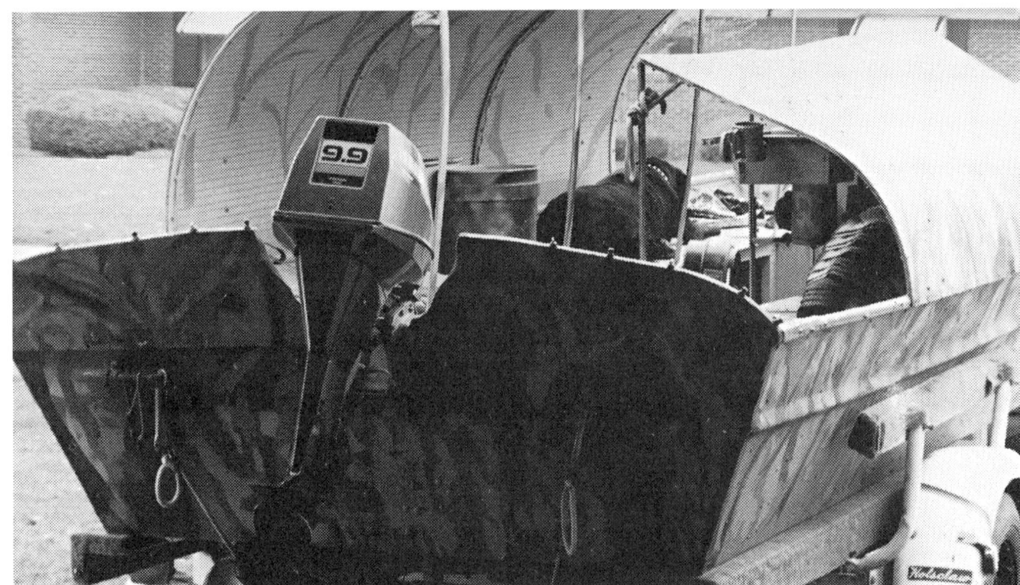

Plastic waste baskets are bolted to the frame of the boat for holding gear, such as flashlights, gloves, hats, and thermos. A five gallon bucket also attached to the framework is used to store extra dry clothing. Three quarter inch pine is used on the bow and stern areas of the boat to build the stern area up, and to attach the canvas covers.

Each headlight and navigation light is on a separate switch and independently wired to the battery with its own fuse. This gives three different (separate) lighting systems.

The transom is elevated to accommodate a long shaft motor. Also, extra 3/4 inch pine wood is used to build up both sides of the motor to enclose the blind.

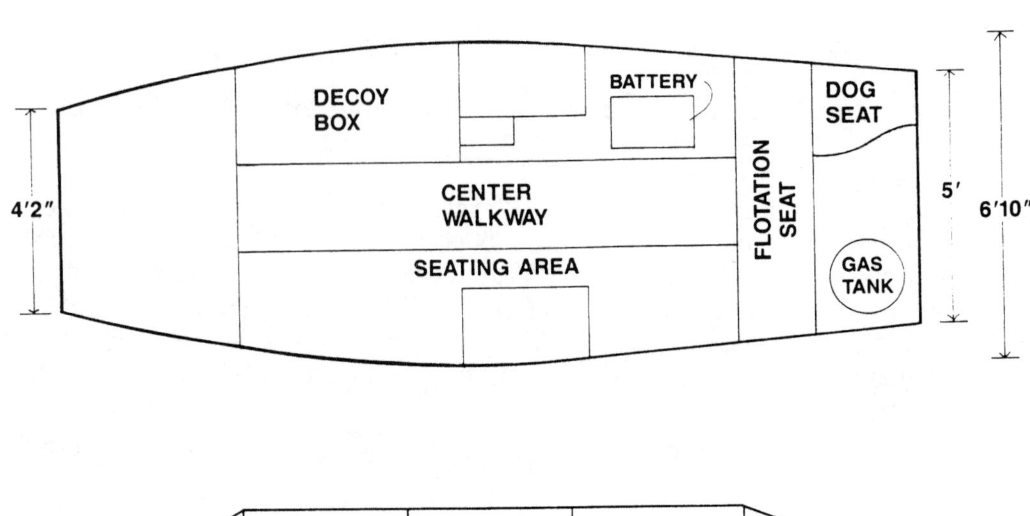
DECOY
BOX
BATTERY
DOG
SEAT
CENTER
WALKWAY
FLOTATION
SEAT
SEATING AREA
GAS
TANK
4'2"
5'
6'10"

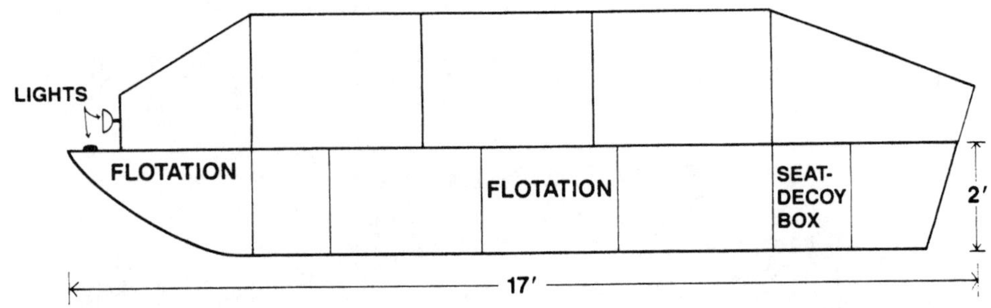
LIGHTS
FLOTATION
FLOTATION
SEAT-
DECOY
BOX
2'
17'

Phillip Carter
West Burlington, IA

Welded Frame Blind

If you prefer a quality designed and constructed boat blind, you will certainly enjoy this one. It is a welded frame blind on a twenty foot, custom built Kann 3/16 inch aluminum plate boat that is capable of breaking ice in the late season. The boat is complete with running lights, spot light, bilge pump, two (16,000 BTU) heaters, stove, and is powered with a 150 outboard.

Construction Notes: Start with 1-1/2 inch angle iron running the length of the boat and a portion of the deck. One inch conduit is installed inside the angle iron. Nine pieces of 1 x 4 inch flat metal are welded on the inside of the angle iron at nine various locations. Using a 5/16 inch drill bit, drill thru the 1 x 4 inch flat metal as well as thru the gunwale. Mark the location of your shooting stalls . Cut a one inch conduit to the height of the front and back of the blind and weld four braces. Next, place (2) ten foot pieces of one inch conduit end to end and weld together. Then place them on top of the two top braces and weld together. Do this for the lower braces as well. Now mark an 18 inch center on the gunwale for front and back side braces. Use 3/4 inch conduit for the sides and cross braces. Make a template for the bends to allow for greater accuracy. After all the side braces are in place, the cross braces are placed between each side brace. Install the the individual shooting stall braces next, again using one inch conduit.

Now you can start working on the deck for the decoy storage. The main frame is one inch conduit and the braces are 3/4 inch conduit. The decoy bin has a top door for easy entry and locking. A small side door allows your retriever to get out of any inclement weather. The decoy bin on this rig will hold 4-1/2 dozen super mag duck decoys.

Place a shelf from the front deck to the wash deck on the front side of the blind. Now frame the motor compartment by framing in door braces. Two shelves constructed from the wash deck to the end of the motor will support two (15 gallon) gas tanks. With all the braces in place, you can start building the doors.

After making the door out of 3/4 inch conduit, weld on the hinges and install them. Each weld is wire wheeled and primed. Now place half-inch plywood on the three shelves. Attach the plywood with one inch self tapping screws. Use .016 roll of aluminum (3 x 100 feet) for the outer shell and attach the shell with half-inch self tapping screws. First cut and place all panels inside the blind. Attach the frames with self tapping screws. The frames are raised above the outer shell to keep the rain from entering. Next, cut the outer shell that will be placed between the shooting stalls. Make the panel two inches wider in order to be able to bend a one inch lip for attachment of a 1 x 3 inch piece of wood for "waterproofing." Now start running the outer shell lengthwise down the boat (front to back). Seal all seams with silicone or other suitable sealer. After the outer shell is complete, cover the door with a heavy gauge aluminum. Install the hasp and door latches. The blind is now ready for priming and painting.

One half inch insulation placed between each brace inside the blind will help keep it toasty warm, and also keep the duck and goose calls from "ringing". Paint the inside of the blind a dark color.

Next, cut and place two layers of camo netting over the blind with U clips and self tapping screws. Place the 4 x 4 inch woven wire over the netting for brushing with natural vegetation. Consider spray painting the wire while it is still in a roll.

Now start making the shooting hole covers. These covers are made of heavy gauge tin, hemmed and cross braced. Place two pieces of 3/4 inch conduit attached to the covers along with 1 x 3 inch framing for bracing. Drill a hole in the middle of each piece of conduit, drilling thru the cover. Place a three inch long eye bolt thru the hole. Make sure the eye bolt is large enough so that a piece of half-inch conduit can be placed thru it. Cut a piece of half-inch conduit four inches larger than the shoot-out opening. Place the half-inch conduit thru the two eye bolts and adjust until the half-inch conduit touches the 1 x 3 inch wood frame. This will secure the shoot-out in place.

Drill one (3/16 inch) hole just above the lower eye bolt and place a cotter key through it. The shoot-outs are locked in place. Camo netting is now attached. This is the time to wire the boat as needed. It pays to have individual switches for each light, and be sure to include a light in the motor compartment. Another option includes constructing a 13 inch x 10 foot long x 20 inch-wide bench with 3/4 inch conduit and 1/2 inch plywood. Brush the blind as needed.

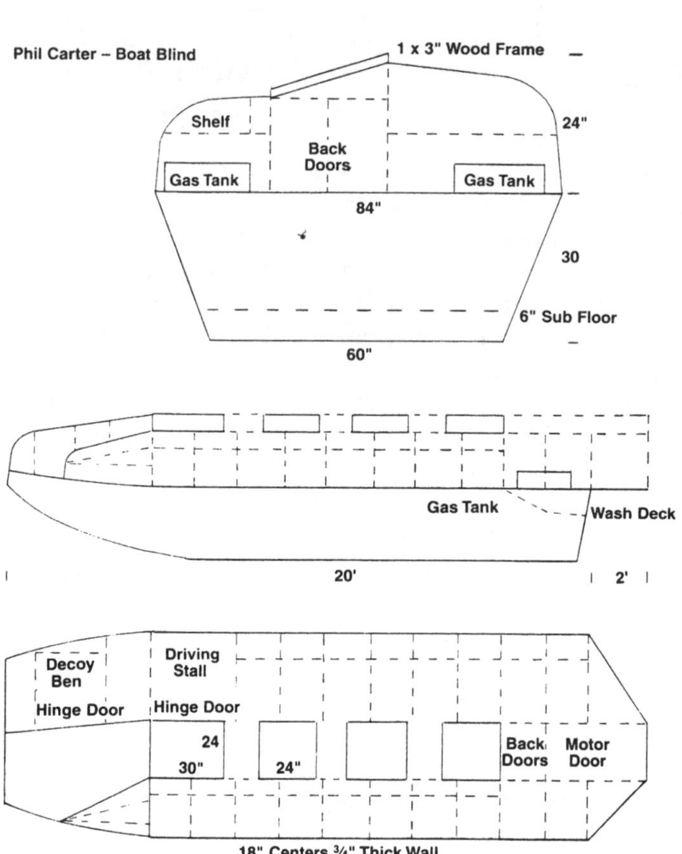

Material List:
*Three feet of 1 inch flat scrap
*100 feet of 1 inch conduit
*300 feet of 3/4 inch conduit
*Ten feet of 1/2 inch conduit
*Two (4 x 8) 1/2 inch sheets of plywood
*75 feet of .016 roll aluminum
*Two (3 x 8) 12 gauge tin
*32 feet of (1 x 3 inch) wood
*Three (1/2 inch x 4 x 8) Blue Board Insulation
*Eight (3 inch) eye bolts
*14 hinges
*500 (5/16 x 1/2 inch) self tapping screws
*Forty feet of 1-1/2 inch angle iron
*Five cans of primer
*Three hasps
*Five tubes of silicone
*Inside lights (as needed)
*Nine (5/16 inch bolts/lock nuts)
*One gallon paint
*Four cotter keys
*50 feet of woven wire
*Inside lights (as needed)

Kevin Ziegler
Apollo, PA

Heated Pontoon

A 24 foot heated pontoon boat, totally waterproofed, complete with lighting, sleeping cots, and generator. Great for open water or marsh. The dimension of this boat is 24 feet long and 10 feet wide; blind is 16 foot by 4 foot high.

Material List:
*17 x 11 foot piece of rubber roofing
*Two gallons of rubber glue
*12 sheets of 1/4 inch ply-score (4 x 8 feet)
*12 sheets of 1/2 inch styrofoam (4 x 8 feet)
*One (4 feet) 2 x 4 for middle roof support
*One (16 foot) 2 x 4 for middle roof truss
*Two burner propane stove
*One 20 pound propane tank
*Three spotlights
*Fourteen metal hinges for roof hinges
*Two pounds of (1-1/2 inch) dry wall screws to attach plywood and 2 x 2s together
*Ten (red) truck lights
*Two gallons of flat black paint
*Two (12 ounce) camo spray kits
*One 110V electric light fixture
*Two 110V electric outlets
*16 foot of #14 electric wire
*Four fold-up cots
*One generator
*Twenty-six (4 foot) 2 x 2s used for supporting sides and roof

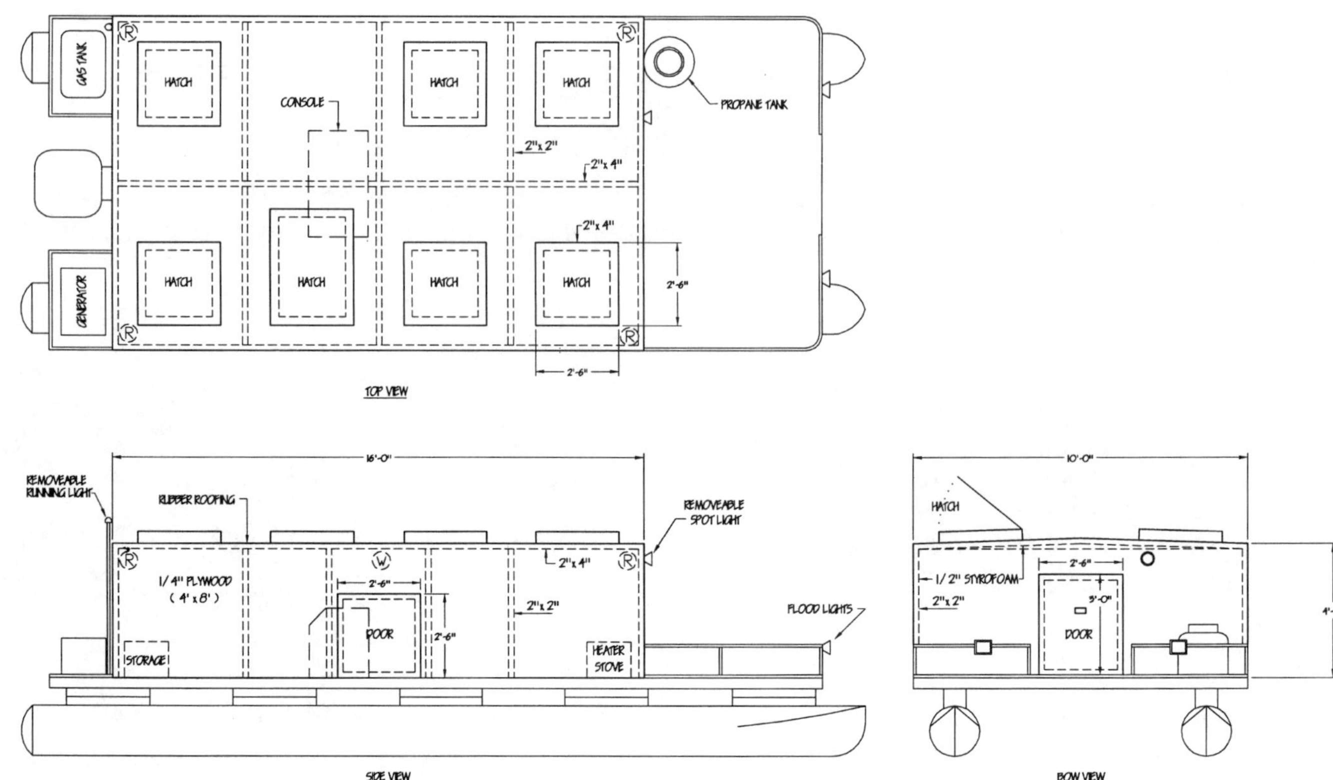

K.Z. FOATING DUCK BLIND
DRAWN BY G.J.G

~ 5 ~
Layouts

The term "duckboat" can mean a number of things depending on where and how they are used. Some duck hunters use the term "duckboat" in the same breath as john boats, canoes, 16' runabouts, and pontoons.

Although some waterfowlers have a problem relating to these kinds of craft for duck hunting purposes, I don't have too much problem with calling them duckboats if properly camouflaged and outfitted for the intended purpose. Technically, however, they are not in the purest sense of the word, a "duckboat." Many would probably be more fittingly called "boat blinds."

This play on duck hunting terminology can also be related to layout boats, for some waterfowl hunters have different ideas as to what is and is not considered a layout boat. In areas that hunters consistently have to deal with heavy water, a larger, more stout boat would be used as a layout boat, one with plenty of freeboard. In a more sublime area where wave heights tend to remain somewhat less of a concern, a more sleek-looking craft may do.

Whatever the case, a layout boat is simply a low profile watercraft that is used to properly conceal a duck hunter in an open water area without allowing the ravages of wind and water to play a prominent role in one's spouse prematurely collecting on your life insurance. The main ingredients for a layout boat are: short length (usually less than 10' in length) and low in statue.

The key in the above definition is the term "open water." Yes, there are a number of boats that can be used to conceal yourself in *open* water. A layout however, not only conceals the hunter, but the craft itself is hardly noticed by low-flying divers; it looks more like a deadfall that floated out to open water.

In the days of market hunting, many of these kinds of duck boats were quite deadly, employing the use of live decoys and heavy swivel guns--actually, small cannons. These battleship-style guns were often mounted in the bow and were usually fired into a flock of flying or sitting birds. Little imagination is needed to figure out how many birds were killed with these weapons. With modern-day limits, a half-dozen waterfowlers could be finished for the season with one shot from a swivel gun.

Fortunately, these guns and the market-style hunting are now history. But the boats still remain, low in profile, appropriately decked to handle the kind of water they are to be used in, and designed internally to provide a reasonable amount of comfort for the hunter.

One of the old time layout boat builders in America today is John Kalash of Gibralter, Michigan. His idea of a well-designed layout boat is one that has a crown that is not too high (like the back of a box turtle), creating a shadow, and not too low which, of course, would be about as seaworthy as a bathtub.

When John heads out to his native Lake Erie on a duck hunt, he may spot what looks like a raft of divers. As he motors toward the birds, he notices a man's head pop up a couple of hundred yards away. "When this happens," John says, "I know the layout boat is well concealed."

There are two basic types or styles of layouts that Kalash builds. One has a slightly higher crown and is called a *pumpkin-seed.* It has a flat bottom and no pit inside which makes it a high rider. This style, according to some, is easier to tow, but is also easier for the birds to spot due to the higher crown.

The second style is a *box* or *pit boat.* As the name implies, a pit is constructed in the bottom of the boat and allows for a much lower profile. Federal law requires that your body must be at least half above the water line. This boat accomplishes just that, but also provides for a boat that blends into the water.

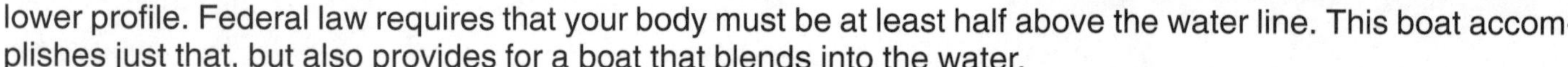

Most layout boats have a canvas cover on top of the boat. This is called a "raise" or "combing" and is used in times of rough weather. Most veteran layout hunters, however, refrain from using the raise unless it's absolutely necessary. When the canvas is put into place, it eliminates the low profile and creates a shadow causing the birds to flare. If the raise is needed, they move it up only about three or four inches, just enough to keep the water from washing over the top. Some layout hunters paint the area under the raise white. This aids in preventing the shadow effect .

Most layout boat builders today feel that the one-man, one-dog layout units are designed about as close to perfection as possible. The two-man units, however, could probably use some modifications in design, especially in areas of making the craft easier to tow.

Those duck hunters who are fortunate enough to live or have a cabin on the waters they hunt are more apt to own and use layout boats. The reason for this is simply that many waterfowlers feel that the work involved in layout hunting is not worth the effort. Instead of hauling 3 1/2 tons of duck-hunting paraphernalia that is normally used by the hunter, layout hunting involves much more gear and, of course, work.

When hunting divers in open water, most hunters have a spread of between 100 to 200 blocks in order to attract the large flocks of divers. There are a few different arrangements for layout hunting. One arrangement employs the use of a "V" design with the layout boat at the narrow or pointed end of the "V." The boat is anchored at both ends, and the wind hovers from your backside as you face the blocks in a prone position.

Normally, the majority of the decoys are strung out between 50 to 70 yards downwind of the boat with a few more on the port and starboard sides of the boat.

The same holds true for the "pearl-drop" arrangement with the exception that the design is, as the name implies, a pearl drop. The layout boat is again anchored upwind, only this time it's at the wide end of the arrangement .

The idea in these two designs is to have the divers fly over your boat, giving you only a couple of seconds to flash a shot at them.

The prone position prevents you from seeing the low flying birds come in at all angles. It's not unusual for a flock to drop in behind you and merrily swim past your boat toward the decoys.

Another method of decoy arrangement is to place several strings of blocks approximately 65 yards long. The decoys are spaced roughly 15' feet apart with four strings on the port side and two on the starboard side for a right-handed shooter. The boat is anchored between the fourth and fifth line about three-fourths of the way upwind from the downwind end of the spread. The idea is to bring the birds down to the left of the shooter in among the decoys.

Although layout boats are most often used in open water situations, they are also used to sneak up on certain species of puddle ducks as well, with much success I might add.

Take, for instance, the black duck. Although the point total for dropping a black has increased significantly in recent years apparently due to statistics that show the black duck to be declining in population, layout boats are often used to produce good results for the hunter who wishes to ruffle their feathers.

It doesn't take long for blacks to become educated enough to shy away from the usual marsh structures that may resemble a blind. Therefore, you must do a certain amount of homework in order to outwit them.

Blacks usually tend to frequent creek areas and small ponds in the evening hours. These areas should be scouted during the early evening to determine if the birds are returning to rest for the night. With a layout rig and a handful of decoys a hunter should move into these areas before dawn and set up.

If you're careful, any birds that may be startled into flight will return in a short time, allowing plenty of action on singles and doubles. It's important however, to allow them to drop well within shooting range for clean kills. As with most ducks, it is much more difficult to finish off a bird in the water than it is in the air. For that reason, if the bird appears alive as it falls, a second shot while it drops may save it from becoming a meal for a marsh predator.

Layout boats were made initially for bluebills and redheads. However, other species may tend to congregate around diver decoys, including goldeneyes, canvasbacks, and scooters. Cans are less likely to decoy in, however, and will circle several times out of gun range, simply teasing the hunter.

If you have never experienced the sport, picture yourself leaving shore in a tow boat with a favorite hunting buddy. As you head out to open water, you spot a raft of divers working about a mile and a half off shore. The adrenaline starts to flow and you look back at the layout rig being towed into position.

The sky is as blue as you have ever seen it, but no matter, open water hunting for divers can be successful any time of the day and in almost any weather condition.

Soon you reach the area that appears to be the most promising and begin stringing out dozens upon dozens of blocks. Your experienced partner gives you the go-ahead to prop yourself in the coffin-style boat in a position you're more used to being in after a four martini evening.

Your eyes gaze up at the clear sky as you listen to your partner move off into some out-of-the-way position so as to not frighten any oncoming birds. He also acts as a standby should winds suddenly produce waves not conducive to layout hunting.

You begin to wonder how difficult it is to shoot from a sitting position in a boat that is bobbing up and down in the one-foot waves; it's an unnatural position for gunning ducks. Nevertheless, your thoughts soon turn to action as a flock of bluebills scream in over the blocks, seemingly low enough to hit with the barrel of your gun.

The only movement up until now has been your heart pumping slightly above the norm and the rolling of your eyeballs beyond the normal periphery of a human, trying to catch a glimpse of an anticipated flock of divers.

The Model 12 pounds against the shoulder and you wonder why you never spent more time on the skeet range. But no matter, as the day wears on and you alternate positions with your partner, one hour in the layout and one in the watch boat, you start to get the drift of it all.

Birds start to drop and soon you are well on your way to

becoming a layout hunter, the peace and solitude only broken by the occasional firing of the gun or the sounds of the wind rushing over the wings of a flock of bluebills. You have arrived.

Work? You Bet! Worth it? Absolutely! It's an experience no duck hunter of any worth should depart this earth without.

Layout Boat Builders

It was not until the 1950's that the commercial construction of layout boats had come into its own. And even in following years, no one made a living producing them due to the limited number of waterfowlers who would choose to use them. Today, there are still a few people who enjoy constructing these units, maintaining a tradition among waterfowlers.

One of these is Sam Devlin of Olympia, Washington. Sam has been professionally building these boats for over 10 years and has several designs available, including a 10' Broad Bill, 15' Black Brant, and a 12' Teal. Prices vary depending on what you have in mind. And if you have the initiative, he will sell you a set of plans to build your own layout. Sam's address is: Devlin Designing, 2431 Gravelly Beach Loop, Olympia, Washington 98502. Phone: (206) 866-0164.

A veteran of layout boat building is John Kalash of Gibralter, Michigan. He has been making the one- or two-man layouts for over 30 years. Costs and availability can be obtained by contacting John at: 30717 Young Drive, Gibralter, MI 48173. Phone: (313) 676-0818.

Lou Tisch of St. Clair Shores, Michigan, has been in the boat building business for many years. His company, Lock, Stock, & Barrell, has a wide line of waterfowl boats, including layout kits. Address: POB 267, St. Clair Shores, MI 48080; (810) 790-2678.

Finally there is Paul Busick with Boats & Blocks by Busick. He can be contacted at 174 Edgewood Drive, Amherst, Ohio, 44001; (216) 988-7160. Kits are available from Paul as well.

Jim Hughes
Cable, WI

Lake Superior Two-man Layout

A large, well constructed "layout" that allows hunters to sit, rather than lay in the traditional prone position.

Construction Notes: Basic construction is marine plywood ribs with cedar strips laid up over the ribs. The cedar is glassed. It is completely enclosed with a sliding top that hides under the deck with a slight nudge. The top slides on garage door hardware. The windshield and side windows are smoked glass, giving only one way visibility.

For the deck portion, locate the longest cedar in stock at a lumber yard without special ordering (usually 18 foot 2 x 6s). This will determine the length. The width is determined by the maximum width (8 feet) that you can toll down the highway.

Rip the cedar into strips. Determine the size of the center bulkhead. Cut a template out of cardboard, sit on the ground and determine the height that would be comfortable for you. Then make the templates out of cardboard of decreasing sizes, going down the nose cone at both ends of the boat. Lay the templates on the plywood and cut them out with a jig saw. Then build the nose cones.

Lay out the three keels and attach the nose cones to them. Set the center bulkhead on the keels and attach it. Take two cedar strips, one on either side and bend them around the center bulkhead, attaching them to the ends. Then set the rest of the bulkheads in place. Flip the rig over on saw horses with the bottom now facing up. Proceed to cedar strip the bottom half of the boat using wide strips on the flat bottom areas. When you reach the curved areas going around the sides, use the more flexible (narrow) strips (3/8 x 3/4 inch). After the bottom is covered, again flip the boat over.

On the top, between the hunter cockpit and the front of the boat, place three cedar 2 x 6s for strength. This area is generally walked on when placing the front anchor out. The part of the boat that covers the hunters is a separate piece of 1/4 inch flexible paneling. It is bent over a headboard in order for a six foot hunter to fit comfortably underneath. For the rollaway top use a piece of half-inch plywood cut to the shape of the hunter cockpit. Use shelf brackets to hold the angle portion of the top on. The forward portion of the windshield is hinged and folds down upon impact.

The next step is to fiberglass the entire boat for strength and durability. The color of the paint is determined by the area you plan on hunting.

There are shelves along each side for hunters to store shells, calls, camera, food, two-way radio, and other accessories.

TWO MAN
LAKE SUPERIOR LAYOUT BOAT

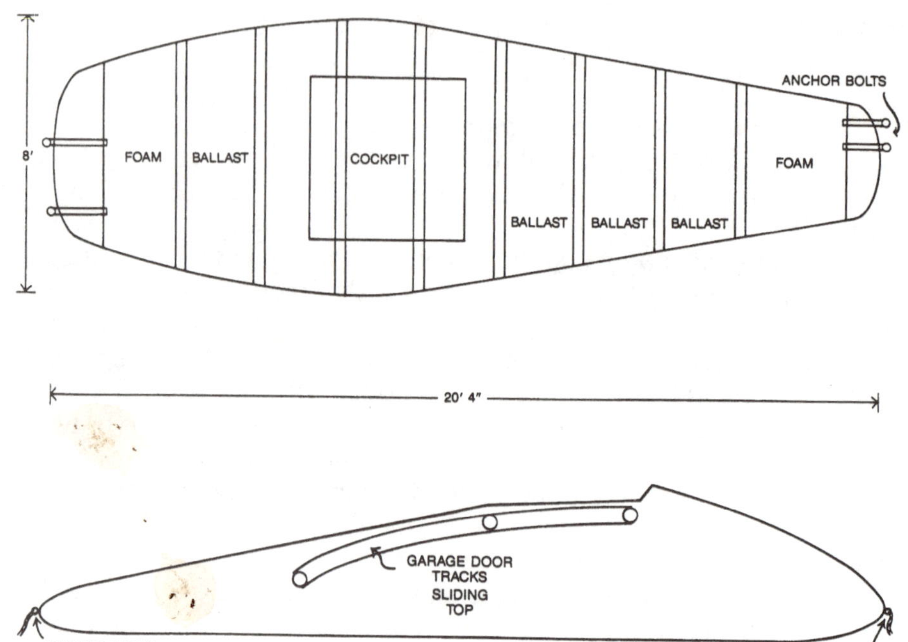

BASIC FRAMING
ONE PERSON
LAYOUT

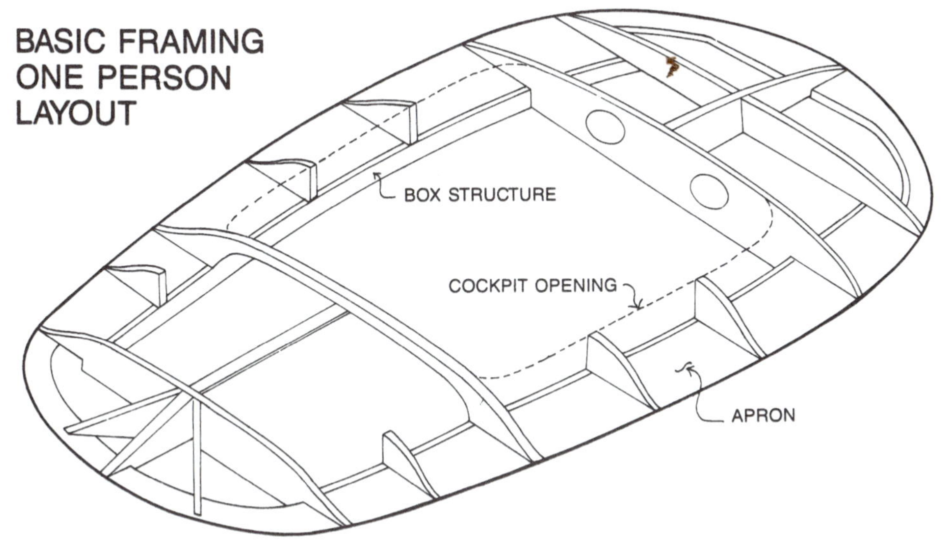

~ 6 ~
Miscellaneous Rigs

Robert Rubino
Merl Salvador
Chester, CA

Submerged Shallow Water Blind

An open water blind that is completely submerged. Used in very calm, shallow water areas (usually less than waist deep).

Material List:
*(2) sheets of marine plywood
*(1) box of 1-1/4 inch flathead screws
*(1) tube of wood glue
*(1) sheet of fiberglass (36 inches x 6 feet)
*(1) gallon of resin
*(10 feet) of 2 inch coving
*(20 feet) of half-inch steel pipe
*(2) overload springs (car)

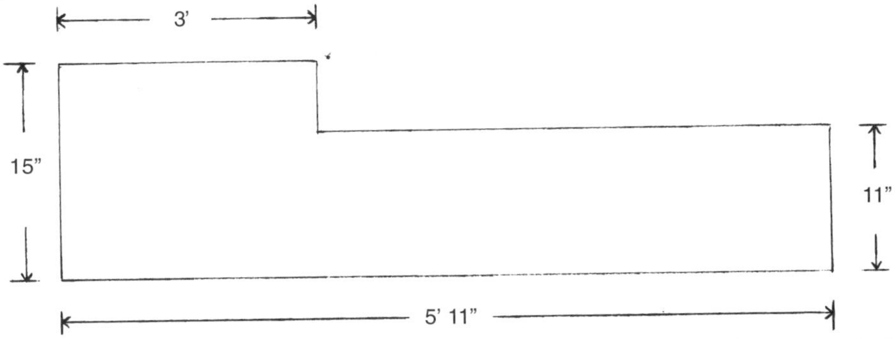

3'
15"
11"
5' 11"

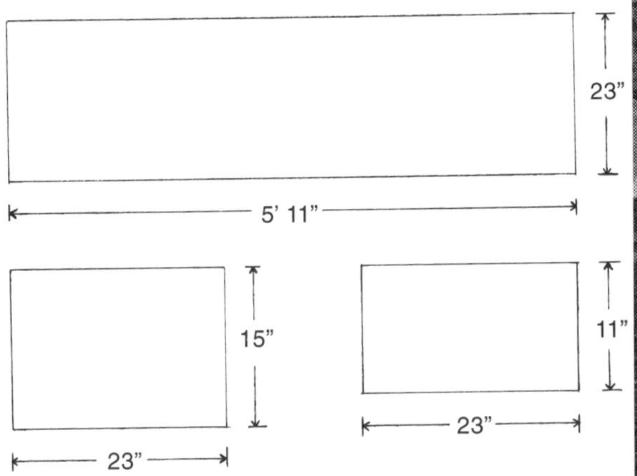

23"
5' 11"

15"
23"

11"
23"

Peter Riley
Shelburne, VT
Don Carpenter
Charlotte, VT

Broadbill Duck Boat Blind

A blind that works well on the Broadbill duck boat, constructed with easily found building materials.

Construction Notes: Aside from the lath stainless steel assemblies on the blind wall which were hand constructed, this boat blind is made with easily constructed materials.

The construction is started by ripping (two) 2 x 8s to contour with the boat cockpit opening. This, being the base of the blind, attach to the boat with (six) 1/2 x 6 inch bolts, washers and locknuts. These bolts protrude through the 2 x 8s via drilled holes to match the 1/2 inch oar lock sockets which are in the cockpit. The boat originally had just two sockets, but four more are added to accommodate securing the blind base. Next cut the pieces of material for the blind walls and assemble them one side at a time. Select your sitting height (usually around 16 inches). The 16 inch height will allow for two (8 inch) panels to fold on top of each other, keeping the blind inside the boat gunwale, thereby avoiding any spray or drag while under power.

Cut and attach two winged panels with two inch square hinges to the front of the blind walls. These will act as support for the front grass panel and also serve as an exit and entry point for your retriever. In the rear (stern), cut a piece of 3/4 inch plywood with eye hooks to be attached to the rear of the blind walls via eye screws. This will support the back grass panel. The grass panels on the roof of the blind are supported by three pieces of 3/4 inch plywood notched the width of the blind walls, making them adjustable. The roof panels not only blend the blind to the marsh, but also will hide the retriever sitting between the two hunters.

Set-up time for this blind is less than two minutes with two hunters, and four minutes with one hunter. This includes adjusting the grass panels according to your hunting situation. While traveling in the water with the blind down, it is held secure with two rubber bungee cords, one on each side of the center area. The opening in the top of the blind when set up is 32 inches for the bow and 34 inches in the stern area. The normal hunting position for this rig is to be seated on a standard folding boat seat which is attached to two layers of 3/4 inch plywood. Both of the seats are now attached to the floor of the boat in order to allow freedom of placement, adjusting to conditions as needed.

This blind allows for hunting from either port or starboard side depending on wind conditions and decoy placement. The top of this blind is only about 30 inches above the water surface, making it very low compared to most boat/blind combinations.

While traveling to the hunting site, decoys are carried loose around the edge of the inside of the boat, and in a bag that is tied down on the bow. With an additional bag between the hunters you should be able to transport at least six dozen decoys. Lumber includes:

***(2) 2 x 8 inch x 8 foot spruce**
***(16 foot) 1 x 2 (# 2) pine**
***(1) sheet of 3/8 inch CDX plywood**
***(6 feet) 1 x 6 (# 2) pine**

Material List:

- *(1) feet) 1/2 inch maple dowel
- *(1) 4 x 4 foot pc 3/4 inch plywood
- *(2 lbs) galvanized drywall screws
- *(6) half-inch carriage bolts, nuts, washers
- *Miscellaneous 1/4 inch stainless nuts/bolts
- *(2) eye hooks
- *(2) eye bolts with nuts and bolts
- *(2) 2 inch hinges
- *(4) 3 inch hinges
- *(4) 3 inch strap hinges
- *(4) custom made latches-stainless
- *(10 foot) 24 inch chicken wire
- *(1 qt) duck boat paint (dead grass)
- *(2 qts) (hunter green & marsh grass)
- *(1 qt) oil base stain primer (brown)
- *(1) boat load of reeds or other grass
- *(6 feet) 14 gauge mechanics wire
- *(10) 7 inch black plastic tie straps

This boat was painted with three colors of Hunter Specialties and Parker paint, all oil base. The reeds were cut in July and weaved throughout the chicken wire, which is very time consuming.

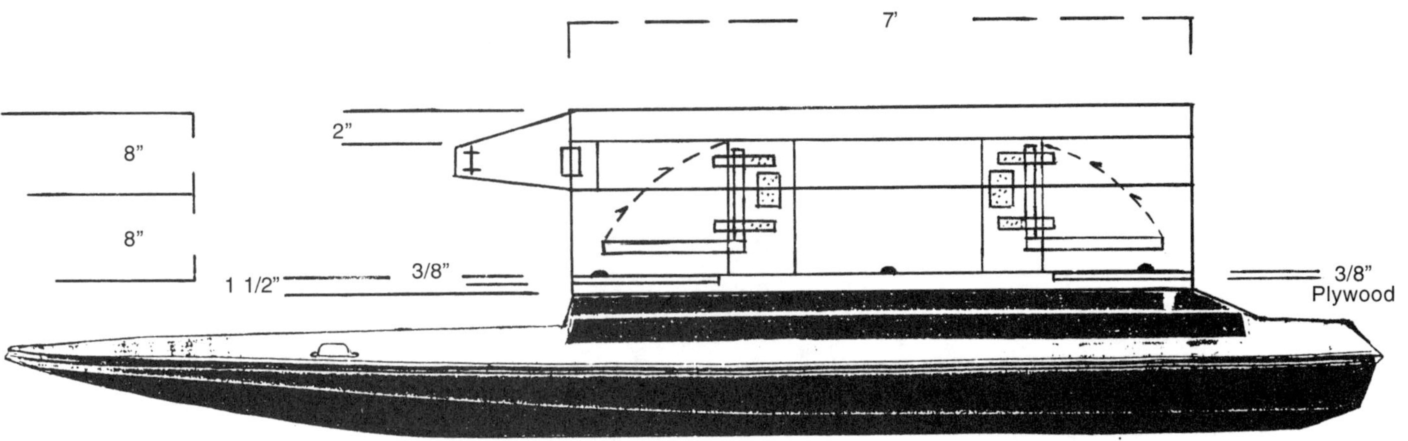

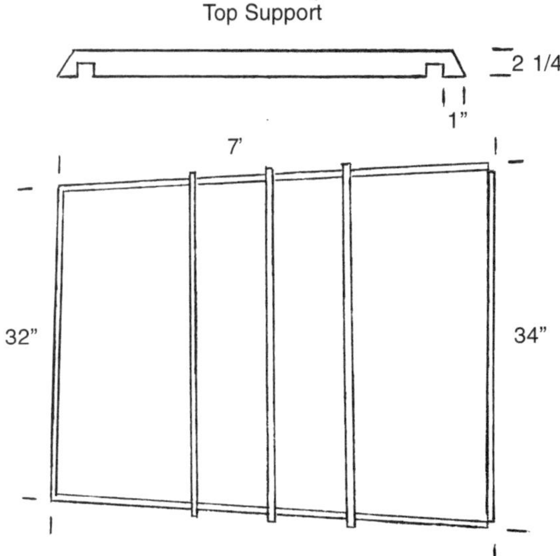

Tom Myers
Carver, MA

Sailboat to Duck Boat

A very creative use of a discarded 14 foot sailboat.

Construction Notes: Getting started may necessitate cutting out the top section of the hull. In order to maintain the length of the boat, the square stern was notched out. Three-quarter inch plywood side pieces will need to be cut and fit into the insides of each transom. The inside pieces and the transom are next glued and fastened to the hull and each other using galvanized sheetrock screws and marine grade urethane glue.

For the sideboards, two inch closed cell foam is used. This particular foam happens to be industrial wall insulation similar to that used in large building construction. The sideboards and front and rear connecting sections are cut and formed to fit in the desired manner. All pieces are sanded to get a rough finish for future bonding to the fiberglass. Vigorous sanding of all materials to be glassed is a necessity. Sanding prior to gluing of the sideboards is the most efficient way to assure complete bonding of the foam and glass.

Next comes the attaching of the sideboards along with the front and rear sections. 3M marine grade urethane glue is used to accomplish this. The foam sideboards have been cut on a table saw with 1 inch deep by 1/8 inch thick grooved 3 inch up from the bottom outside of the sideboards. The groove is pushed over the top edge of the fiberglass hull. This allows the glue to be fully utilized on all inside and outside surfaces of the bonding joint. After the sides have been glued, braces are installed temporarily to assure that no gaps between the foam and fiberglass occur. Allow the glue to cure for at least 72 hours at 70 degrees; longer during cooler periods.

Now it is time to fiberglass the sideboards to the hull, the transom, fill in the centerboard hold and put an extra layer of glass on the bottom for added hull integrity.

If the grain appears to be going in the wrong direction for the required transom strength, cut the top section off and add two full length layers of 3/4 inch plywood. Each is glued and screwed to the remaining section of the transom. Now glass over it for more strength and wearability.

Along the bottom outside of the hull, add two wooden stakes for better directional stability. Again apply glass to cover these additions.

On the outside of the hull, a brace is added for structural strength along with a brace for the forward back rest. Then the console is added as desired. Three quarter inch plywood on the front and bottom are glued and screwed to the side boards. Three eighths plywood is glued to the top, then a layer of cloth and resin over the entire console.

Before painting, vigorous sanding is needed. This cannot be overstressed as the failure of the paint to bond to the fiberglass can leave a white spot shining through. Paint an appropriate color for your hunting area.

With the addition of some final items such as backboards, gun racks, added floatation in the bow and stern, paddles, poles, anchors, cushions, camo netting, motor covers, etc., you are ready to go.

Material List:
*Stake length on bottom...10 feet each
*Foam length...10 foot on top each side (10 feet x 2 x 14 inches)
*Wood...White Oak for stakes and braces
*3/8 inch and 3/4 inch CDX plywood
*Glue...3M Marine Urethane (5 tubes)
*Fiberglass cloth...20 yards x 38 inch of 10 oz
*Resin...3 gallons of Arcon 250
*2 gallons of Arcon 200
*Hardener.....as needed for above resin
*Screws.....1-1/4 & 3 inch galvanized sheetrock
*Paint...1 gallon camo (mixed to suit taste)
*(1) six inch cleat
*(2) 1/4 inch eyebolts
*(2) gallons of Acetone thinner

FORWARD VIEW FROM STERN

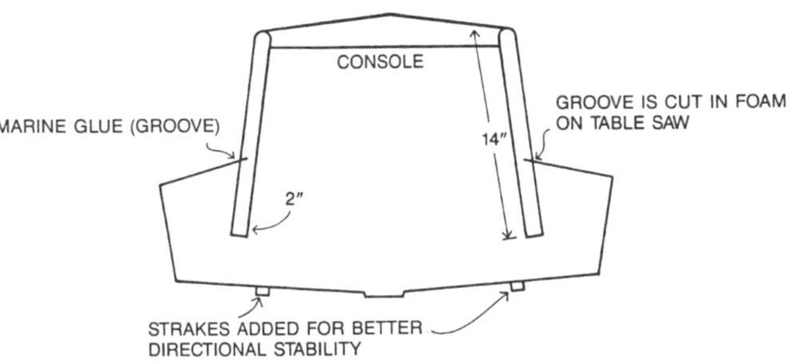

Boat L.O.A.: 14 foot stem to stern
Width: 52 inches
H.O.A. 23 inches
Weight (bare hull)...approximately 150 pounds

Brian Hartman
Mohnton, PA

Sixteen Foot/Low Profile Cedar Strip Construction

A sixteen foot, stable, low profile boat with large capacity for hunting in open water. Capable of hunting three people, this boat is planked for lightness, with a mere 3-4 inch draft, and 950 pound carrying capacity.

Construction Notes: The hull is constructed of cold-molded white cedar strips (1/4 x 3/4 inch), random length, and then lightly glassed. Other materials include white oak, white ash for the stern board, white pine and marine plywood for the ribs. The center cockpit divider/ seat and back rest has a waterproof storage hatch for cameras, emergency gear, dry clothing, etc. Wiring for the lights and other electronic gear is run through PVC pipe.

Construction costs were not bad at $500. But the time to build this rig is approximately 200 hours, which is equivalent to five normal full time work weeks. The finishing touches included cleats, grabhandles, shell and thermos holders, raised floor boards with slats for drainage, and a lot of pride.

When hunting from the shoreline, a small amount of grass or brush is all that is needed to conceal this boat. When in open water anchored amidst the decoys, the low profile and high degree of stability makes for very comfortable shooting.

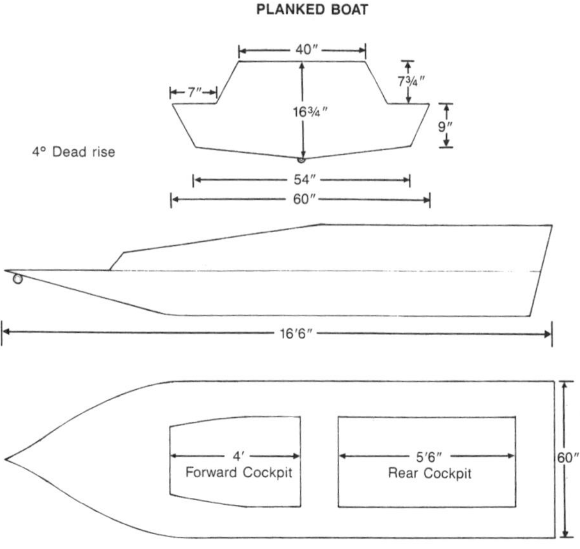

John Bucklin
Machipongo, VA

One-Man Rig Made From One 4 x 8 Sheet of Plywood

To celebrate the purchase of a new saber saw, John decided it would be an interesting project to see what kind of boat he could build out of (essentially) one piece of (4 x 8) plywood. Too bad John did not purchase a buzz saw. Maybe an ark would have been in his future.

John's first effort came out looking like a western steelhead drift boat, and was useful only if you weighed in at less than 50 pounds. So he decided that his next attempt would need to be flat, and as wide and long as possible if it were to be anything approaching stability. This would require minimum waste (probably even using the sawdust), something that could be achieved only with square lines.

With a minimum of eight inch sides for starters, John then selected a square stern and bow; the only curve would be where the bottom was steam-bent in a parabolic arc to meet the forward mini-deck. This would allow for easier paddling or pulling. The small deck could have been eliminated, but it added rigidity, something that generally would be lacking in a small boat. Construction is relatively easy for this rig, except for the bending of the plywood.

Eventually after a trial run, John decided that this boat was seaworthy and rigid, at least in shallow water areas. The size also allowed him to add his 85-pound setter. Fiberglassing added weight, but also provides more overall strength.

This size boat for shallow water and one person allows for ease of transport, can be pulled over mud or low water conditions, can be used to lay-out in low vegetation, and works well for towing extra gear/decoys. It is relatively stable, but John suggests to not shoot or stand when afloat since it is not stable enough under those conditions.

Sculling

Sculling is an age-old traditional method of waterfowling that dates back to the market hunters, and has a proven history of success. In a scull boat, each hunter lies low in the boat. The back hunter, or helmsman as they are called, propels the boat with an oar that extends from the cockpit through the stern, and the front hunter waits to get in range of a sitting flock of birds. It's kind of like jump shooting, but you have the advantage of keeping low in the water in order to gain valuable distance before jumping the birds. If you are in to taking your camera along, often you may get close enough to various waterfowl to take excellent photos.

The helmsman propels the sculling boat by twisting in a figure-eight motion, moving the oar blade enough to propel water backwards and the boat forward. It's a very quiet, effective technique of waterfowling, working well in the marsh, open water, or on a stream.

It helps to scout a body of water first, glassing for rafts of birds, then moving in from an upwind position. As you move within range the helmsman pivots the boat to get both hunters into shooting position. Some hunters even work a scull boat with a layout rig. The scullers work area rafts of birds, keeping them in the air in hopes they will work their way to the position of the layout.

There are very few sculling manufacturers around the country. One manufacturer that offers a kit is Lock, Stock, & Barrell, Inc., POB 267, St. Clair Shores, MI, 48080; (313)790-2678, fax 790-2653.

~ 7 ~
Getting From Here to There

Along about midway through the duck season, could the interior of your car be mistaken for a wetland area? Does your wife need to wear waders and rubber gloves when she drives it grocery shopping? If so, then an alternative method of hauling your duck gear may be in order.

Duck hunters have come up with a number of contraptions for hauling all their duck-hunting paraphernalia to and from the marsh.

A pickup truck outfitted with a topper works quite well for keeping the marsh from entering the cab. Some hunters customize their pickups to include separate storage areas for the gun, dog, decoys, motor, clothes, etc. Others simply organize their trucks about as well as a four-year-old's toy box.

A common method of hauling hunting gear is to place it all in the boat and pull it behind your car or truck on a trailer. This usually works quite well, and in most cases is an ideal method, especially if a larger boat is used for your hunting.

For those of you who would like a small summer project, one that will make your hunting much easier and your family vehicle more acceptable for hauling Mom and the kiddies off to grandmother's, then the following unit may be just what the doctor ordered.

Simply stated, the method of transporting all of your hunting gear that I'm about to describe in detail consists of a 4 x 8' box (or some other suitable dimension) placed on top of a small boat trailer or other acceptable type of trailer. It has enough room to store several dozen decoys, motor and gas tank, waders, paddles or oars, life preservers, and almost any other item that you take along with you. The box can be locked and secured in place, and on top goes your canoe or other small watercraft.

Everything is placed on or in this hunting box, and it can be left as is throughout the season. When you're ready to go hunting, you can easily hook up to the trailer, grab your dog and favorite hunting companion (which may very well be your dog) and you're off. No more forgotten waders or gas can. No more searching for your canoe paddles at 4:00 a.m. They're always in the box.

I keep referring to this set-up as a "box," but credit should be given to its originator whose name is Larry Griffin, a long-time Michigan waterfowler. I suppose we should rightfully call it "Griffin's Box."

Basically, Griffin's Box can be constructed with (four) 4 x 8' sheets of 1/2" plywood, a few 2 x 4s and a gallon or so of an appropriate paint.

Start out by obtaining all of the materials listed above, as well as some good wood screws and a bottle of wood glue. Wood screws hold much better than nails and should be used since this unit will take quite a pounding on the road.

Another item that may be added to the overall planning of the construction of Griffin's Box is the off-season uses such as hauling wood, top soil, or your kid's stereo to the dump. By incorporating a removable top with the use of latches, it can be used year-round, making it easier to justify economically.

On the other hand, if you have a small fishing boat and trailer, the box is all that is needed. If you plan on using the trailer only in conjunction with the box, look for a good used trailer or a sturdy used axle, preferably with large tires, and then custom-make the frame. Remember to use a long tongue, especially if the back of your car swings open. Room must be provided for the area between the box, boat, and the back of your car or truck doors.

The exact number of 2 x 4s will be based on the type of cradle used on the trailer. This part will be custom made due to differences in trailer styles.

On a boat trailer, a few judiciously placed "U" bolts will secure it. But plan to run the "U" bolts through the bottom of the box in such a way as to intersect a 2 x 4 and anchor it down using the wood supports as a securing point.

The half-inch 4 x 8 sheets of plywood need only be good on one side. The inside of the box can be rough. Cut one of the 4 x 8s into two 2 x 4 foot sections and another into two 2 x 8' sections. Seal the sides of all the 4 x 8s that will make up the inside of the box; it's much easier to take care of this step now rather than when it's completed. You may also wish to paint the bottom of the box at this time. Be sure to use a good water sealer of some sort. This is critical since the box will obviously be wet during much of the hunting season.

After the inside parts of the box have been painted, including any support pieces, the assembling comes next. You may want to assemble the bottom 4 x 8 sheet on the trailer, line up all attachment points, and drill the holes accordingly, and then take it back off and work on the box on a flat surface.

Use 2 x 4s around the inside bottom of the box as a framing structure. This includes the perimeter of the bottom as well as a 2 x 4 across the 4' center of the bottom. Use 2 x 2s for the vertical corner supports and for framing the inside of the top piece.

Originally the doors on this box opened to the sides, but after some adjusting, it was discovered that doors that flip up on top of the box were easier to work with and tend to stay out of the way when loading and unloading.

A vertical 2 x4 in the center of the side where the doors are located will provide added support to the doors. Two 4' doors are better than one door. Remember to use the wood glue on all pieces that will be put together, such as the 2 x 4s, and 2 x 2s. Run a line of glue the full length of each support piece. Also, be sure to place heavy duty hinges (at least three per door) and good lock latches on the doors.

A narrow compartment (approximately 12" wide) at the front or back of the box is ideal for storing your motor and gas can. You may wish to custom frame the compartment to cradle your motor for easier riding. A small shelf above the motor could be used for paddles and other miscellaneous items.

As a final construction note, place a five-foot 2 x 4 across the top front and back of the outside of the box and slightly above it so that your boat rests a couple of inches higher than the top of the box. A five-foot 2 x 4 is used in order to have room for more than one canoe, should the need arise.

Next, set your boat on top and proceed to place four eyebolts at each of the four corners of the boat where it meets the 2 x 4s. These will provide anchor spots for the boat tie-downs. Again seal and paint the finished product the color of your choice. Finally, add appropriate lights for driving purposes.

Before you run out to the nearest lumber company, give this box some thought and you may eventually come up with modifications that better suit your needs. Whatever the case may be, this type of trailer unit without question makes the trip to and from the marsh--and storage between trips--a much easier and more enjoyable adventure.

Trailer Ideas

~ 8 ~
Repairing/Hardware/Painting

Dealing With "Dry Rot"

With the advent of fiberglass and epoxy technology over the past couple of decades, our attention seems to have been diverted away from wood and wood related problems. But actually many of our fiberglass boats have wood cores and much of the older technology has not provided indefinite protection of the wood from problems such as "dry rot". Through years of use in adverse weather conditions screw or nail holes tend to take on water which eventually works its way into the wood and starts the rot process. Damaged fiberglass also adds to the process of rot with the eventual outcome requiring repairs of some magnitude. Many times our initial thought is to scrap the boat and start over. But there is hope in most cases and many problems such as dry rot can be overcome.

The problem with "dry rot" is that it works like a cancer, often times going unnoticed until significant damage is done. According to the WEST SYSTEM® Technical Manual, "dry rot is the best known problem with wood and is caused by fungal growth." Actually the term "dry rot" is misleading since moisture must be present for the rot fungi to exist.

Even though there are many different types of rot fungi, there are two main species in the brown rot family that are the primary attackers of wooden structures. And in order for these two species to survive, four conditions must be present:

1)The moisture content must be at or near the fiber saturation point (rot is unknown in wood with a moisture content below 20%).

2)There must be an adequate supply of oxygen.

3)The temperature must be warm; 76-86 F (24-30 C) is ideal for rot fungi, but they have been known to be active in temperatures as low as 50 F (10 C).

4)There must be a proper kind of food (wood fiber).

"DRY ROT"

If any of these four conditions is missing, fungi cannot survive. Past efforts to control brown rot have generally centered around poisoning its food supply. Most of the commercial wood preservatives use this approach, but they have had only limited success with respect to boat hulls.

When a boat reaches the rot condition you will need to make a decision on whether or not it's worth saving. But don't be too hasty with your decision. A few hours, or at best a few days of work, could result in a boat that is almost as good as new.

I once had the opportunity to rennovate a layout boat that had been neglected and eventually developed a fair amount of dry rot. As weathered as this rig was, I had a feeling that it could be resurrected. Before I proceeded with this project however, I took the boat to Gougeon Brothers in Bay City, Michigan. Technical experts like Brian Knight, J. R. Watson, Jim Derck and others are part of a large staff that specialize in epoxy technology.

After looking at the condition of the rig, Brian Knight echoed the feeling I had, stating that it was worth salvaging. The boat was in relatively sound condition and with about three or four days work I figured I should be able to make it look at least respectable. And it might even float.

Gougeon Brothers has a manual titled "Wooden Boat Restoration and Repair" (available for a small fee from a WEST SYSTEM® dealer or from Gougeon's direct). The manual addresses the feasibility of restoration or repair and the potential use of the WEST SYSTEM epoxy; analyzing the structure for loss of stiffness and dry rot damage, and preparing for work; repairing techniques for small areas of dry rot; replacing and repairing damaged frames, beams and keels; hull and deck planking repairs if applicable; installing hardware with epoxy in order to increase the load-carrying capacity of the hardware and eliminate deck leaks; protecting against UV, finishing and maintaining your finished product.

If you want to get really technical, there is data in the appendix that discusses the percentage increase in wood strength properties for every one percent decrease in moisture content for various woods; mechanical properties of various wood species commonly used with WEST SYSTEM Brand Epoxy (relative strengths), and other interesting information.

Commonly asked questions dealing with key steps in repair and restoration, inspecting and locating damaged areas, safety, handling epoxy, basic techniques, drilling, filling, reinforcing, joint repairs, working with plywood, bonding hardware, painting, repairing dings and cracks, and ventilation (for longevity) are all addressed in the publication. It's well worth acquiring this manual if you plan on doing any work on a wooden boat. An address is listed later in this chapter.

Tips on Bonding Boat Hardware

When bonding hardware such as a cleat or eye hook, spray the hardware with Pam. This will provide a non-stick surface on the screw end of the hardware allowing for easy removal after the epoxy cures. Also, it helps to heat the boat surface to allow the epoxy to "draw" in to the fiber.

Extending Resin Work Time

Increasing the surface area of the epoxy/resin mix will extend the working time. The larger surface area will draw off heat quicker from the epoxy, thereby slowing the curing process. You can extend the working time even more by placing the resin/hardener mix in a plastic pan and setting it in an ice bath. This again will draw off heat from the mixture.

Removing Old Hardware

If an old hardware item has been previously bonded in epoxy and you need to remove it, heat will do the trick. At temperatures above 150 degrees F, cured epoxy begins to lose its physical properties and will soften. Heat the item with a soldering iron or propane torch. Be sure to protect the area around the hardware from heat damage by covering it with water-soaked plywood. After the heat is conducted through the base of the hardware, the resin softens and a sharp rap with a mallet should dislodge it. If it doesn't break easily on the first try, heat it a second time and try again.

Refurbish Your Old Boat

Continuing on with the refurbishing of the layout rig, I started with the tedious, but important task of stripping the old layers of paint and glass. This was accomplished with a belt sander and coarse sandpaper. This process will do a fairly good job, but heating with a torch and scrapping the warmed finish proved to be quicker. I enjoy finish work, but prep work to me is about as enjoyable as open heart surgery. The heat and scraping method however, made this task much easier.

After removing a reasonable amount of the old paint and fiberglass, proceed to sand the boat down to the bare wood. After the majority of the old finish is removed, concentrate on the layout cockpit area.

The floor in the cockpit had severe dry rot and instead of repairing it I decided to cut it out and replace it with new wood. I used a 4x8 foot sheet of basement grade, treated plywood. This is an expensive piece of wood, but being that the cockpit is a critical area of the boat, subject to severe moisture problems, it was important to spend a few extra dollars for a quality piece of wood. The vertical sides of the cockpit were sound so I cut only the flooring out of the boat. Cardboard was used to cut a pattern from the hole in the floor. The cardboard was then transferred to the treated 4x8 sheet of plywood and used as a guide for cutting the finished product.

The bottom was then screwed on from the side as opposed to using nails. Nails were used by the original builder of this boat and consequently the structure did not hold up as well. It is also critical that all screws be properly sealed to prevent moisture from entering and allowing the start of rot.

Gougeon's manual states that the forces acting on a boat during normal use places each joint under a continual strain. For example, when a wave or swell passes under a boat, it lifts the hull unevenly. Waves supporting the hull under the ends force the sides of the hull apart; a wave supporting the hull in the middle forces the sides together. Waves or swells crossing at an angle can lift the bow in one direction and the stern in another, causing a twist that pulls one side of the hull and deck forward and the other side aft. Other loads come from lifting the boat for storage or adding cargo. Thus, a boat is under a constant state of twisting, stretching and flexing. All of the joints must resist this flexing to keep the structure rigid and watertight.

The smallest movement around a fastener can weaken the fastener's holding power, leading to more flexibility. Over time, every exterior joint that can flex is a potential source of moisture penetration. Traditional caulking methods are intended to flex and absorb the movement between adjoining pieces, but with the continual flexing, these caulking materials will eventually break down. Without regular maintenance, the caulked joints will leak. Then, high moisture content of the wood around the joint leads to loss of wood strength, loss of fastener holding power, more flexibility and even more moisture penetration.

The hardware should receive the same thorough attention that the deck has received. To overcome problems associated with hardware installation on wooden boats, Gougeon Brothers, Inc. has developed an approach called "hardware bonding." As the name implies, hardware items are bonded to wood with the goal of distributing high, single-point loads over as large an area of wood fiber as possible, while allowing the epoxy to seal and protect the wood end grain exposed by the fastener hole.

There are two ways to do this. The first is to bond all fasteners (screws, bolts or threaded rod) directly to the surrounding wood fiber. The second is to bond both the fasteners and the hardware to the immediate wood fiber on which they rest. Using proper hardware bonding installation techniques, you can dramatically improve the load-carrying capacity of your hardware rather than using standard hardware installation methods.

In saltwater applications, experience shows that bonded hardware and fasteners give excellent resistance to corrosion attack. Where fasteners are vulnerable to flexing and saltwater attack (i.e., hollow or bridged traveler tracks, bonded U-bolts or solitary eyebolts), a small silicone sealant fillet covering the joint between the cured epoxy and the fastener will protect against moisture and salt intrusion. Of course, any exposed metal surface will be subject to the effects of saltwater corrosion, and therefore proper maintenance and cleaning procedures must be practiced.

All of this may sound a bit complex for your duck boat, but with the little extra effort you can add years to the life of your rig. Once you discover how to properly restore the boat, the actual techniques are not complicated.

After the bottom of the layout boat was replaced I needed to fill the areas where dry rot had invaded. For this process I used an epoxy mix of low-density filler and colloidal silica. The filler is mixed in with the epoxy and the silica is added as a thickening agent. Thickness can be controlled by the amount of filler and silica added to the epoxy.

An unthickened mixture with a "syrup" consistency is fine for coating or "wetting out" surfaces, but for filling holes or gaps it's best to have a "peanut butter" consistency. A low-density filler mixture is used because it is easily sandable. High-density filler mixtures are strong, but are hard to sand, and are used in structural applications like bonding, filleting and hardware bonding. The epoxy filler mixture hardens fairly fast so sanding can take place relatively soon after the initial application. Once the sanding is completed you're ready for the clean-up and the glass work. Clean-up is simply a matter of washing down the boat with clean water. This is a must in order to remove any sanding residue.

Next the fun part, glassing the boat. I am not going to go into any detail on this procedure because it's lengthy and is spelled out in Gougeon's Technical Manual. What I will say is that applying fiberglass cloth to a boat is not difficult. Actually it's relatively easy and enjoyable. At this point in the refurbishing process you start to see the boat take on a "new life". It's like adding a new body to a car. Your are actually sealing the wood structure, and preventing moisture from causing damage to the wood fiber.

I used a lightweight (4 ounce) glass cloth on my layout because I wanted to keep the weight down as much as possible. I don't need the glass cloth to add strength to the boat so the 4oz cloth will work fine. The main emphasis here is to provide a suitable barrier between the wood and any moisture that comes into contact with the boat.

In the areas where strength is needed, such as at the seams, I used Biaxial Fabric to reinforce them. This 15 ounce fabric comes in a roll, generally 4 inches wide, and is used around all the seams both inside and out.

Since the newly installed bottom was basement grade treated lumber, I did not fiberglass this part. I simply applied a coat of epoxy to act as a sealant, thereby providing more protection. After the fiberglass cloth has been applied and the epoxy dries, the final step before painting is to lightly sand any rough spots and wash with clean water. This is important due to a by-product of the epoxy curing process called "Amine Blush". Amine Blush appears as a wax-like film on cured epoxy surfaces, and must be removed. Fortunately it is water soluble, and can be easily removed by washing with water. If not removed, it will clog sandpaper and inhibit the bonding of paint.

Refurbishing your old wood boat is not as difficult as you might think. The processes are relatively easy, and with a few spare hours or days, your rig can look as good as new. And, with today's new epoxy technology, your boat will probably last longer then when it was new.

If you want more information on epoxy technology, products, brochures, or cost, you can write or call Gougeon Brothers, Inc., at P.O. Box 908, Bay City, Michigan, 48707, (517) 684-7286, Fax (517) 684-1374.

Painting Your Duck Boat

Any duck hunter who has spent at least a couple of years in the business has more than likely purchased a new or used watercraft of some sort. Subsequently, he/she probably has been faced with the infamous chore of painting it. It's not really the painting part that becomes a problem, but rather the preparation that must take place prior to the final finish coat.

One thing I remember about purchasing my first canoe is that I had it painted dead grass green by the company I bought it from. The reason was simple: They would heat treat the craft, providing a hard, tough finish that I felt would not peel like most homemade jobs. The extra cost is worth it.

One of my first aluminum boats did not offer the option of a manufactured paint job. Therefore I took it upon myself to make the shiny craft resemble the color of the marsh that I frequent during the fall duck hunting season.

My first step was to discuss this matter with a friend, a professional painter who paints everything from bridges to water towers. I figured if anyone would give me some sound advice about how to proceed, he would.

After consulting with my friend, I started on the task with renewed confidence. My instructions were to start out by etching the surface of the canoe with coarse sandpaper. The problem with aluminum is that it is difficult to make the paint stick. By the very nature of the metal, aluminum is very smooth with little adhesion qualities. Sanding gives the paint a "surface" to grip and hold without peeling.

Most people don't know that aluminum, like stainless steel and iron, does corrode. When iron, for example, oxidizes, it produces what we commonly call rust; aluminum does exactly the same. However, it "rusts" so fast that it produces a film or layer which then protects it from further corrosion.

So in order to create a good "holding" surface for the paint, this corroded layer must first be removed just as rust needs to first be removed from an iron surface.

There is, however, an alternative to sanding. It's the use of acid-containing primers called vinyl-wash primers. If all the steps are followed in proper sequence using these acids, vinyl-wash primers are a good way to prepare the surface for the top coat. It's probably slightly better for underwater use, as opposed to sanding. However, if the steps are not strictly adhered to in the time restrictions stated on the directions, there can be a problem with delamination between the vinyl primer and the top coat. Most top coats are conventional solvents, meaning they are paint thinners or mineral spirits and do not have a lot of "bite" to them. Therefore, timing is critical so that the vinyl primer does not harden before the top coat is applied.

For these reasons, I personally prefer the sanding method. And by using a mechanical sander, the job is far from difficult. I used a 5/8" drill bit with a sanding attachment and completed the job on the 15-foot Grumman in less than a half-hour.

My next step was to paint on a coat of bonding elasimer. This product provides a good bonding surface for the top coat. It's a relatively expensive clear liquid, but fortunately very little is needed for the job since it spreads easily on the metal surface. Other bonding primers, such as marine vinyl zinc chromate also work well.

The final step is the top coat in the color of your choice. I preferred to spray on the top coat making the process much faster and giving it a uniform, professional look. I highly recommend this method over a brush.

If you have a boat constructed of steel, such as a old pontoon boat, you may need to treat it somewhat differently compared to aluminum. Brand new steel has a residue that is formed during the manufacturing process called "millscale." You may have seen movies or pictures of the inside of a steel mill where a roll of steel is moving along a line and sparks are flying through the air and then dropping back down on the roll. When the pieces of steel are sailing through the air, they pick up oxygen. When they fall back down, they form a thin layer on the steel called millscale. The steel now has a slightly different potential to rust as opposed to the regular steel underneath this layer.

As a result, this millscale layer must be removed in order to provide a profile in which the paint will adhere. A good way to do this is by first sandblasting the steel. If the boat has been sitting out and is rusted, sandblasting will again be the preferred method of removing the rust. On the other hand, if the steel has a layer of millscale and sandblasting is out of the question, then the option is to let the steel set out and produce its own layer of rust. What happens is that the original steel will not necessarily rust, but the millscale layer will Then, with only a light layer of rust, you can remove it with a hand wire brush or power brush. You will then have a nice, clean surface to work with. But remember that letting the craft rust naturally may take six months or more. Sand blasting is obviously much quicker.

Next, apply a rust-inhibiting primer and then your finishing coats. We could go into all kinds of ideas for the use of rust-inhibitor primers for there are many on the market, some being much more expensive than others. For all practical purposes however, use an alkyd base preferably one with a barium compound in it like barium sulfide.

It is much better to put two coats of primer and one finish coat as opposed to one primer and two finish. The extra primer coat (getting as much of the steel covered with a product that has reacted pigments in it) is strongly recommended. The finish coat simply makes it look nice and produces the color you want. It also adds some wearing properties to the boat, but will, in time, need to be touched up.

If you have a boat made of ABS plastic and want to paint it, the process is quite simple. Sanding is the first step to remove the gelcoat layer and provide a dull surface. Then a fiberglass primer is placed on the surface of the boat. A couple of finish coats and you're done.

Remember to sand the plastic, because the gelcoat layer acts the same way as the millscale and must be removed. At that point, the plastic will be quite porous and rough and will need to be sealed with an appropriate primer.

Now for new wood. Wood in the natural, unfinished state is also fairly simple to protect from the ravages of nature. The important consideration is to give special attention in the moisture-proofing process. Not just water-proof, but moisture-proof. While the paint will water-proof, you need to go one step further, that is, to apply a wood preservative which does two important things. One, it will provide a fungicide/ mildicide to keep down the possibility of dry rot, and two, it will provide water repellency. These wood preservatives usually are organic-type materials. Do not use anything with silicon in it, because this will prevent adhesion of the paint. Soak the wood well with the preservative and let it dry. Choose your wood presertative with care; the best marketing program does not always mean the best preservative.

The next step is to put a good wood primer on the boat. Let it dry and then lightly sand it to remove rough spots and bumps. Finally you finish off with at least two coats of a polyurethane boat enamel in the appropriate color. That's it.

Refinishing a used boat depends on the condition of the boat. Most paint products continue to "cure" or oxidize over a long period of time. As they cure (age) they have a tendency to lose the adhesive power and become brittle. Therefore, if you purchase a boat that weighs less than the paint on it, you will need to strip it back since the paint layer is no stronger than the weakest area, and you have no way of knowing where that area is.

No matter how many coats of paint you place over the old surface, if the adhesion lets loose underneath, your new paint will also come off. If the boat is in the condition just stated, or if you can see that at least one-third of it is peeling, your best bet is to strip it down to bare wood and start over.

The best method of stripping old paint is to use heat. Heat guns are excellent and do a very thorough job. They are also a lot less messier than chemical strippers. However, on plastic and metal, the chemical strippers are the only method to use.

If you decide to use a chemical stripper, there are a number of good ones on the market. Generally speaking, get one that will take off epoxies and polyurethanes because these paints are more difficult to remove and more resistant to standard or conventional strippers.

The important thing to remember with strippers is to use a sprayer if possible (even if you must use a garden sprayer) rather than a brush, and allow it to do the work. Let it sit on the surface for the recommended period of time and even a bit longer. Then take a small knife and scrape a section back in order to determine how well the remover is working.

Most removers are designed to form a "skin" and will continue to work if left undisturbed. Once disturbed, the methylene chloride will evaporate and it will stop working. If you must use a brush, don't "over-brush." Over-brushing will immediately break the skin and prevent the remover from doing the job you purchased it for; that's why spraying does a much better job.

For your top coat, always use an oil base paint--never a latex. Latex paints are a relatively soft coating in comparison to an oil base and will not give you the abrasion resistance you need for a duck boat.

During my days in the marsh I have seen duck boats that looked like they have not been introduced to a good coat of paint since the days of 25-bird limits and market hunting. Remember:

Your duck boat comes next in line behind your retriever. Treat it well and you will have two friends with you the next time you head out to your favorite hunting location. Neglect it and some day it may 'let you down.'

~ 9 ~
Tips & Ideas

Adjustable Motor Mounts

Always keep in mind when you build or purchase a new waterfowl rig that it will pay dividends to provide some means of allowing you to raise or lower your outboard. At the very least, you should be prepared to elevate the transom mount by adding a piece of metal or thick wood. This will help in shallow water or weed areas that we often encounter. Look at some of the commercial units.

Aerial View of Blind

I once hunted with a friend who had a permanent blind in a local cattail marsh. At first sight the blind appeared to blend in well with the surrounding habitat, but after the first week of hunting he had very little luck decoying birds into his spread. Finally he decided to look at the blind from the birds' perspective. He rented a plane for a half-hour and flew over the blind. From the air he noticed the trampled cattails around the blind, giving away his position. A second thing he discovered was that the interior of the blind was not as well concealed as he initially thought, allowing the ducks to easily see any movement by the occupants. Actually this idea of flying over your blind before the season may prove worthwhile for making some previously unnoticed corrections.

Always Anchor Your Boat

I have heard more than once where someone has left the confines of their boat to set out decoys only to soon find out that the boat drifted away. Some have even died due to drowning (not necessarily duck hunters) when their boat drifted too far and too fast to get back to it safely. Always drop an anchor whenever you leave your boat, even if it is for a brief moment. This simple habit could save a lot of grief.

Binoculars

Never leave shore without them. A pair of binocs can be a great asset for locating distant birds working another field or water area. Scout an area before you head out by scanning the water or field to see if birds are in the area. If not, move to a different location and try again. Many times I have saved myself the effort of setting up decoys in an area only to find out that the birds are working elsewhere.

Boat Wheels

If you hunt in an area that requires some overland travel with your boat, you can save your back and legs by providing some type of roller device or wheels for the boat. The one method I have seen used is to mount a set of wheels on the sides of the transom. Most of these methods have been of an individual design, none being identical and most being radically different. The primary concern is to make sure the wheels are firmly mounted, using rivets or strong stainless steel bolts whenever possible. Another consideration is to make sure the wheels can be adjusted to be able to keep them out of the water when motoring to your hunting spot. Permanently mounting them below the water line will result in unnecessary drag in the water.

The above method is fine for some people, but personally I use a method that consists simply of purchasing a piece of 2" diameter rigid plastic pipe and cutting it into lengths of approximately 24". Black or grey pipe is best since it's less visible to the ducks while stored in the boat. When you need to pull your boat over dry land, lay each section of pipe across the area you wish to pull the boat over at approximately 8'-12' intervals. You now have a simple, easy method of moving your boat even full of gear. I use four sections of pipe and move them ahead of each other as needed. Ancient Egyptian history and the use of such rollers for moving huge blocks of stone for pyramid building have taught us a useful lesson.

Boat Pullovers

If you regularly hunt an area that requires you to drag a loaded boat over a dike, you can assist your back by installing pullover devices at the location you pull the boat over the dike. These can be a very simple device such as 2x4's strapped together, or a more "sophisticated" roller type construction for the larger, steeper dikes. Either method will make hauling your boat over dikes much easier. I have even seen some very steep dikes use a combination of rollers and a small pulley system mounted on a solid stake at the top of the dike. With this type of setup, one person can haul a fully loaded boat over a dike with relative ease.

Boat Storage Idea

Plastic waste baskets are bolted to the frame of the boat for holding gear, such as flashlights, gloves, hats, and thermos. A five-gallon bucket also attached to the framework is used to store extra dry clothing.

John Bendzsa,Terre Haute, IN

Bungee Cords

It's always a good idea to include the use of bungee cords in any waterfowl boat/ blind design. They provide great means of attaching natural camo material such as cattails, evergreen branches, or grasses as noted on the photo of the Outlaw boat. Use two rolls of bungee material if space allows to keep the camo material from shifting. Also note the natural grasses used on the Outlaw which are the same as the background habitat.

Camo Idea

A durable material that works extremely well for camouflaging is baling twine, used for baling straw. It can be cut in short lengths and tied to another rope extending around the gunwales. The rope should last for several seasons.

Cold Weather Safety

It's no secret that cold water conditions can quickly kill should you become immersed for even a short period of time. A life jacket alone will do you little good under these conditions. Hypothermia sets in quickly and can kill you before help arrives. The best defense for getting yourself out of such a life threatening predicament is to plan ahead. If you hunt big, open water, don't risk your life over a limit of ducks if the weather is bad. Wind and waves are deadly, and even more so when the water is close to turning hard. Duck boats, no matter what size, are not made for these conditions. Overconfidence in your boat, reliance on your past hunting experiences, or your over zealous love of waterfowling in these conditions can spell BIG TROUBLE. Tomorrow is another day to do what you put off today....but lived to tell about it.

Color Blind

Color blind doesn't refer to our keen-eyed waterfowl friends, nor does it have anything to do with your eyesight or mine. Color blind refers to how we tend to use different colors, either solid or in combination, and how they may relate, or blend, to the surrounding environment.

When we finish the construction stage of that "perfect" waterfowl rig, the next, all important step, is to provide a suitable color that will help conceal it from the high flying waterfowl. Ideally we try to imitate a surrounding habitat; i.e., cattail covering in a cattail habitat, or corn covering in a cut cornfield. That usually is a snap for most waterfowlers.

In open water however, it is not so easy to conceal. The color of water can and does vary considerably, depending on many conditions, including natural light, clouds (or lack of), bottom soil texture, and depth of the lake or bay you are hunting. Bottom soil texture refers to sand, silt, or clay that make up the bottom soil. If a body of water is shallow and contains light sediment (silts/clays/fine sands) it will tend to take on a different color when riled by boats or wave action. We have no control over these natural occurrences, only the color of the rig we are using. If you hunt open water, and primarily in the same area, you can try to imitate the color of that body of water. Even the best of color schemes cannot always be ideal, given different environmental conditions.

Water tends to take on or reflect the color of the sky. Cloudy days generally reflect shades of gray. Sunny days will be different for that same body of water. An early ice-up will again change the color of the water surface.

During one particular waterfowl season, I took two layout boats, each a different color, on a large body of water to determine how they may vary in different light conditions. I also attempted to take aerial photos, although trying to line up several hunting buddies on a moment's notice, along with a plane and pilot at the same time was no easy task. There were days when the lighting conditions were ideal (dull, cloudy), but wind and other factors made it impossible to fly and take good photos.

Toward the end of the season I managed to fly over my two layouts, but the sun was shining and the water developed a thin layer of ice the previous night. After hunting the first hour or so, I headed to the airport, a mere half-hour drive from our hunting location. It was no easy task heading back to shore a mile away through the ice, but I knew that this would be my last chance to shoot photos for winter was arriving early this year in the northern states.

Once over the bay, it was easy to see how the color of the water took on a completely different tone from the week earlier when ice was absent. The ice allowed the water underneath to "settle down"; all the fine sands settled out and the water cleared. The sandy bottom, which normally goes unnoticed in open water conditions on this particular bay, now reflected an entirely different color. Especially with the existing bright light conditions. If clouds would have been present, I'm sure the ice would reflect the off-gray tones that normally make up these conditions.

One layout boat was painted the "normal" light to medium gray; the other, a drab olive with streaks of black intermixed. The drab olive was easy to spot from the air, and even in open water conditions, it was evident that you are usually at a disadvantage with drab olive. With the hazy sun, even the gray could easily be distinguishable. Sun is a killer to layout concealment.

There are no all around color schemes that can be used in all open water conditions. It's a crap shoot. You paint for the ideal conditions, and leave it at that. The traditional light to medium gray will work as well as any on layouts or low profile open water boats. Then pray for cloudy days and moderate winds.

Commercial Blinds

There were at least seventy five commercial boat and blind manufactures in the U.S. and Canada at the time this book was published. Many have some very fine rigs that will fill your needs no matter whether it's in the field, marsh, or on the open water. Several are listed in this book. It is nice to be able to have the time and resources to build your own rig, but everyone simply cannot. That is where the dedicated waterfowlers who decided to create a commercial boat or blind can fill your void. Most of these companies are small operations; some are a sideline to a larger company. Look to them for ideas, products and assistance.

Cutting Fiberglass

When cutting fiberglass material, it is helpful to use a carbide-tipped saw blade in a saber saw. This method helps keep the dust to a minimum and is easier to control. Don't forget to wear a protective dust mask, goggles, a long-sleeved shirt, and barrier cream on your upper body.

Larry Fry
Poway, CA

Decoy Bag Safety Device

Keep in mind that a decoy bag, complete with decoys, can make an excellent flotation device if you're swamped. They WILL NOT replace wearing proper flotation devices, but can assist in saving a life or keeping your boat afloat should the need arise. If you have the habit of placing all your decoys loose in the boat, you may want to consider placing several in a decoy bag and strapping the bag to the boat.

Jack Visuri
Saginaw, MI

Decoy Retrieval Tip

An easy method of retrieving your decoys without leaning over the side of the boat is to purchase a 6' long 1 x 2 or 2 x 2 and attach a three or four-inch long hook on one end. As you move alongside your decoy spread, you simply use the pole and hook to grab the anchor line of each decoy and pull it in. This idea works especially well when the wind makes it difficult to maneuver your boat out in the open water.

Drilling PVC

Before gluing a plastic elbow to a pipe, fill it with a mixture of sawdust and epoxy. When it hardens, the mixture will enable you to drill holes into the elbow. The epoxy and sawdust mixture provides a solid support base.

Jim Bambenek
Winona, MN

Electronics

With today's modern era of electronics, several pieces of equipment are available to make your hunt easier, more enjoyable, and safer. One is the Global Positioning System (GPS). The handheld units are great for locating your hunting blind in the dark, or getting back to your vehicle from the flooded woods or marsh. They are inexpensive, and well worth every penny spent. Another piece of equipment that I use religiously is a pair of walkie-talkies. They are terrific to communicate with your partner in a layout rig, keeping in touch with friends who may be hunting in the area, or when you must leave a blind to retrieve a bird in tall grass or heavy marsh conditions. A marine radio or CB can also assist you when you are lost or weather conditions start to present a problem and you need help. These handheld units may even save your life.

Equipment Hauling Tip

If you're like most duck hunters I know, your small boat is probably rated for a maximum of 650 pounds total for equipment and occupants. Usually though, it has somewhat in excess of 900 pounds going out to the blind and another 150 pounds coming back, including 100 pounds of excess water in the bottom of the boat and 50 more pounds of water in your waders. Much of this can be avoided by towing along a small 12' canoe or rubber raft of some sort. The additional watercraft can be used to store your bags of decoys and other bulky items that take up much of the available room in your boat. Usually you can find a used canoe or small rubber raft at garage sales or by placing an ad in the newspaper. For around $100 or less, you can make your hunting trips much easier and safer.

Five Gallon Pail for Storage

A good method of keeping your shells, food, extra clothing, and other small items dry while hunting is to get a five-gallon pickle pail with a cover and use it to store and carry all your items to and from the field. Paint the pail an appropriate camo color.

Extra Clothing

Always set aside a spare set of dry clothing at the beginning of the season and take it along on each and every trip. If you're like me, sooner or later you will need it as shown in the accompaning photo of a friend who fell out of a canoe while hunting.

Floorboards

Even if your boat doesn't leak, waterfowlers know that the bottom of most boats seem to accumulate water as the day progresses. Floorboards will keep the inch or so of water that tends to enter the boat from coming into contact with the gear that you intended to keep dry. The key to helping prevent a slippery floorboard is to give them a heavy coat of paint or epoxy and sprinkle them with sand before they dry. The sand gives the floor finish a rough texture, thereby helping to prevent slips. Another idea is to glue indoor/outdoor carpet (dark grey or other acceptable color)to the wood flooring. Dark grey paint mixed with sand is brushed on the front and back upper decks. The sand gives the surface a non-slick finish.

Pam & Troy Biddle
Terre Haute, IN

Flooring in Boat

If you use a solid wood flooring over the top of your boat floor, drill several 3/8 inch holes in the wood to allow water to flow to the bottom of the boat.

John Bendzsa
Terre Haute, IN

Gun Mounts

There are numerous gun cases for waterfowlers on the market, many of which I have yet to actually experience how practical they may be. Some claim they float with the gun inside, others are simple Cordura coverings that provide some level of protection while moving from shore to blind. Whatever you use however, it is advisable to keep your gun secure in the boat, whether it is in a case or not. One idea that seems to work well is to secure two of the foam lined gun holders on the ends of the seats in your boat. The gun can easily be placed in the security of the holders, and is readily accessible.

Gun Protector

An easy, inexpensive method to keep your gun barrel from becoming scratched on a metal boat is to purchase foam pipe covering from a hardware or plumbing shop and attach along the gunnels. This will help keep your gun from sliding and scratching the barrel, and also helps keep the noise of banging gun barrels against the gunnel to a minimum.

Gun Safety

During the planning stages of blind construction, always keep in mind a place for your gun(s). A "v" notch cut into the side at some point will keep a loaded and therefore potentially dangerous gun from falling and possibly discharging. I personally have witnessed the fortunate return of two hunters from a hunting trip with a gaping hole in the side of their boat due to just such an accident. The shotgun of one of the fellows had discharged upon falling into the bottom of the boat, letting in a gob of daylight through the port side. They managed to stick rags and shirts into the hole and limped back to the parking lot. When constructing a water blind that is subject to freezing water conditions, keep any camo brushing above the highest water line since the weight of the frozen water could disturb all the brush from around the blind. Keep in mind that aluminum boats are not only noisy, but abrasive as well, and can remove the bluing from your gun. Either tape your gun barrels or place a protective cover over the metal.

Hinged Shelving

Shelves are handy to have in a blind, but are sometimes not always used or needed. Therefore when constructing shelving, add piano hinges to allow them to be folded against the wall. This will allow more room in the blind when the shelves are not being used.

Michael Eckery
Lincoln, NE

Keeping Blind Supports Afloat

Filling blind supports and crossbars with spray foam will keep them floating if dropped overboard.

Larry Fry
Poway, CA

Ladies Camo

I am seeing more and more woman waterfowlers out in the marsh. Until recently however, not much was available in the line of camo clothing for woman. Companies like Columbia Sportswear, Orvis, and L.L. Bean have a fine line of ladies clothing, but two individuals have specialized in this area, especially in the camo line. No need to wear an oversized man's pair of pants or jacket. Contact Suzy Smith at POB 185, South Fork, CO, 81154, (719)873-5121, or Vickie at Zanika, 4315 Oliver Ave. N., Minneapolis, MN 55412, (612)521-1429 for a catalog or listing of where their clothing lines can be found.

Lasting Memories

Be sure to take a camera along on your hunting trips. I relive many experiences in the marsh while sitting home in front of a warm January fire. Taking good quality photos with a 35mm camera can be more of a challenge than pulling the trigger on your Model 12.

Layout Board

For the waterfowler who hunts a variety of field habitats on a limited budget, the layout board might be worthwhile considering. It is portable, comfortable, effective, inexpensive, and, best of all, easy to construct. It can be used in corn fields, tidal salt grass marshes, or along lake shores/creeks/drainage ditches.

Materials: Sixteen inch x eight foot (half-inch, 5/8 inch, or 3/4 inch thick) plywood.
One (1 x 4 x 9 inch) back support brace
Two (1 x 1 x 6 inch) braces for back support brace
Two (two-inch) hinges
One foot of rope

Directions: Cut two feet off the end of the piece of plywood for the back rest. Hinge the back rest to the remaining six foot piece of plywood, placing the hinges on the bottom of the back rest and toward the short end; the hinges should be about 20 inches in from the end. Tack one of the (1 x 1 x 6 inch) braces on the end of the six-foot piece of plywood centered under the back rest. Position the other piece of (1 x 1 x 6 inch) wood centered on the bottom of the back rest and a slight distance from the top so that when the back support brace is in place the incline of the back rest is in a comfortable position. Attach the (1 x 4 x 9 inch) brace to the layout board with "U" nails and rope. Paint as desired.

Don Kay & Bob Vellucci
Hampton, NJ

Locating Fixed Blind

Not everyone owns, or even intends to own a GPS to help locate their blind. In the dark locating a blind can be difficult, especially the first few days of the season. One method to help locate your well camouflaged blind is to place a couple of reflectors, or use reflector tape on the front of the blind. A spot light will quickly pick up the reflectors in the dark.

Bruce Pussehl
Saginaw, MI

Mini-Light

Working in the dark, whether you're unloading the boat from the trailer, or setting out decoys, can be difficult. You can simplify matters by purchasing one of the small night lights used by flyfishermen. They attach to your shirt or jacket and have a flexible goose-neck-style head, allowing you to direct the light where needed. This small, yet handy light source can be used any time the need arises, and is one of the handiest waterfowling gadgets I use.

Natural Camo Material

It pays to try to use Mother Nature's natural camo material whenever feasible. When hunting in a cattail marsh, use at least some cattail for cover. Attach some to your boat or blind to help blend in with the natural surroundings, but be careful not to cut the camo in big patches next to your hunting spot. Cut sparingly and keep the area as undisturbed as possible.

Paddle Notches

Notches filed on the sides of your paddle blade are handy for snagging decoy lines. Also, paint one paddle a fluorescent red on one side to be used as a visual signaling device in case of an emergency.

Larry Fry
Poway, CA

Paddles

When selecting paddles for your boat, don't skimp on size or quality. Waterfowl hunting is often very demanding on man, machine and equipment. A paddle should be tall enough so that if you get yourself into a situation that you need to stand and paddle (shallow water conditions), a longer paddle will come in handy. Select heavy duty ash paddles, not the soft pine type. Ash will give you many more years of service. Some of the plastic paddles may work well under warmer conditions, but I have busted them in temperatures that are near or below freezing. Although I have personally not experienced it, I have been told that varnish can give you blisters with steady use. So you may want to sand it on sthe handle end, and repaint with a camo color. Wrapping with tape may also help prevent this condition.

Ivan Mothershead
Charlotte, NC

Permanent Open Water Blinds

Many hunters have permanent blinds on bodies of water that rise and fall as the tides or winds dictate. You can construct your blind above the highest known water level, or design your blind to "float" as the water levels change. One method to accomplish this is to run your support posts through the corners of the blind, but do not attach them permanently. Let the blind "ride" up and down the posts as the water levels change. This will keep your blind lower to the water, making it easier for entering/exiting and dog retrieves. Drilling holes through the posts will allow you to stabilize the shooting platform at a set height.

Fred Wahls
Freeland, MI

Polyester Mesh

When working with polyester mesh (nylon line) try burning the line instead of cutting; this will help avoid fraying the material.

Portable Boats

Everyone doesn't have the availability of a truck or trailer to haul the necessary waterfowl gear from home to hunting site. One of the solutions that I have seen used to overcome this concern is to obtain a portable boat such as the popular Porta-Bote of Mountainview, CA. A lightweight polypropylene model is manufactured for waterfowlers, complete with a squareback design and hunter green color. You can fold this unit up to four inches flat and can easily mount on top of your car. Check the ad listing in the commercial section of this book for brochure information.

Pre-Planning Your Boat Layout

While in the process of designing or constructing your boat or blind, keep in mind whom you are designing it for. Are you tall or short, a left-handed or right-handed shooter? Do you prefer sitting with your back to the side of the boat or blind, or do you prefer facing the length of the boat? What about your retriever? Where does he or she sit while waiting for your command to fetch? Be sure to look closely at other designs and then add your own requirements or personal preferences.

Preventing Rust on Conduit

When using conduit for your blind frame, consider painting and wrapping with burlap to prevent rust and minimize the need for repainting.

Mark Fincel
Columbia, MO

Punt Pole

For years I have seen a hunting buddy of mine take along with him on most every hunting outing a 10' long pole with a 'V' shaped piece of metal attached to one end. He called it a "punt pole" or "push pole." I soon realized how valuable these simple gadgets are for attempting to move through flooded woods or water lily choked marsh. When props clog up and paddles are difficult to use, these poles are the next best thing. When you push these poles down in the ground beneath the water, they are designed to fold out and keep the pole from driving into a muddy bottom. When you pull the pole up, the "rabbit ear" bottom folds back together, allowing the user to pull them up with ease. The 'V' shaped bottom unit can be purchased for around $10 from many catalog dealers such as Gander Mountain out of Wilmot, Wisconsin, or Wing Supply of Greenville, Kentucky. The catalogs usually refer to these units as "duck feet" or "mud lickers."

PVC Rollers

Several pieces of two foot long heavy gauge plastic pipe spaced approximately five feet apart on the ground will allow you to easily pull a several hundred-pound boat over dry land.

Raised Boat Motor for Weeds

Duck hunters, for obvious reasons, will frequent areas that have thick growths of aquatic plants, both submerged and on the surface. Therefore, unless you are one of the fortunate few who own an airboat, the vegetation has a way of making it difficult to motor from point A to point B. One way to assist your motor from becoming less of a burden and more of an asset is by elevating the transom on your stern to allow the motor shaft to ride higher in the water. This can be simply accomplished by bolting a couple of pieces of 3/4" plywood on the stern, just high enough to keep the prop at a minimum depth. Keep in mind that when the boat is filled with hunter, dog, and various other gear, it will ride lower in the water; therefore, you must allow for this when determining the elevation needed for your particular rig.

Retriever Platform

An idea for a dog platform for the floor of a canoe is the use of a plywood board cut to fit the contour of the inner area of the canoe. The board only needs to be approximately 30" long by whatever the width of your canoe is. The board will provide a dry area for your dog to sit on and a good platform to jump from when you give the fetch command. Some hunters go one step further by placing a piece of outdoor carpeting on the platform. It gives your dog that much better footing, but is not really necessary.

Retriever Platform/Ramp

There are numerous excellent commercial retriever platforms on the market, or you can customize one for your boat or blind. It is much easier on your dog and yourself to invest the time and/or money for a ramp or platform.

Retriever Safety

When hunting in areas that support the growth of bamboo-size brush, be careful not to cut these off in the area where your retriever may be leaping in after a fallen duck. A dog could become impaled on one of these pointed objects. If you are hunting in an area that you are unfamiliar with, and appear to have similar type growth, check out the area around your boat or blind before you begin hunting.

Retriever Training Opportunities

Having a slow day in the marsh? We all have them from time to time. Here is the ideal opportunity to work your retriever as the author works his labrador, Maggie, in the adjoining photo. Always take along a training dummy (other than your hunting partner) to work your dog during those slow moments. In addition to the workout, a dog swimming around the decoys on a calm day will stir up the water and help attract attention to your spread.

Safety Feature

One idea that works well for gun storage, is to secure two of the foam lined gun holders on the ends of the seats in your boat. The gun can easily be placed in the security of the holders, and is readily accessible.

Safety Gadgets

About the time the waterfowl season starts to near the end, I like to start thinking about the next season; at least with respect to some of the gear I thought I could have used and didn't have, or the numerous items I took out in the marsh and never used, and probably never will. Waterfowlers tend to have at least one of everything, many times two, and usually a backup. We are easily identified as waterfowl hunters simply by looking in our garages.

One of the areas that I find we may be lacking is in that of safety equipment. Simple little devices like a compass could turn a potential disaster into a lifesaving situation. I carry a compass in most every hunting coat I own. That way, if things get a bit turned around I can at least head in the right direction, especially as nightfall approaches. I have had my share of unpleasant experiences in flooded woods, and for that matter upland woods as well. I would probably carry a compass to the jon if it didn't seem so absurd.

Another small item that could prove valuable at times are a couple of flares, maybe even one of the inexpensive flare guns. You may never use them, but if you need them, you will be glad you packed them along.

Spare dry gloves, socks, and stocking hat to protect sensitive areas of the body may also prove useful at times. I prefer wool, since it keeps you warm, even when damp or wet. If it's Gortex lined... better yet.

A simple first aid kit, extra flashlight batteries, binoculars, a set of tools for basic engine repairs, extra spark plugs and shear pins will help round out your safety equipment. A set of tools alone can come in handy when you find a fellow waterfowler that did not have the foresight to take his own along, and is now adrift in the middle of the marsh. You could probably rent them out enough times over the course of a season to guys like this and pay for a year of college at an Ivy League school. All of this stuff put together doesn't amount to much financially or in terms of space. But when the time comes to use any, you will be glad you have it.

Sunrise/Sunset

Although a sunrise is beautiful to watch, it can be difficult to shoot waterfowl when directly facing a bright eastern sky. Be sure to keep this in mind when setting up your blind location.

Swamp Seat

Swamp seats can make life a bit easier in shallow water. A simple, yet useful gadget to provide a resting spot for yourself between flights. A four foot long 2 x 4 with a 4 x 8 piece of wood attached to the top will allow you to rest in a semi-seated position. Some waterfowlers tend to get fancy by attaching bar stool tops or other similar contraptions for the seat portion.

Towing Lightweights

Packing too much gear in a boat can be uncomfortable and outright dangerous. Try pulling one of the lightweights, such as the famous Poke Boat on your next trip. That extra gear can easily be towed to your hunting site and then the boat can be used to make retrieves or adjust decoys. They're also nice to get to those out-of-the-way places. I have used mine extensively during the season for hunting, as well as off-season for floating streams for steelhead or small pond fly fishing.

Tie Down Posts

If you hunt shallow water areas, an inexpensive and easy method to turn an unstable boat into a stable shooting platform is to purchase two screw-in type dock posts with a cross beam. Screw the posts into the ground next to the center of your boat, place the cross beam over the two posts and tie together. You now have a stable platform for shooting.

Towing a Boat

When towing a small boat, keep most of the weight in the back of the boat. This will keep the bow up and prevent it from zigzagging back and forth in the water.

Water Bailer

A simple bailer can easily be made from a square plastic gallon paint thinner jug. Attach a wooden handle to it and you have a handy bailer. The flat side picks up water much better than a round can or jug.

Larry Fry
Poway, CA

Winch

A winch on your truck can be a handy piece of equipment. Dragging your boat back to the truck across a muddy area can be tough on the body. Use it to pull out all the shrubs around the house so you won't need to trim them during hunting or fishing season. They are a helpful tool for more than just pulling your truck or someone else's out of the ditch.

~ 10 ~
Canoe Technology

(Note: Although this article pertains to materials, dimensions and shapes of double-ended canoes, it can be applicable to square backs, and to an extent to boats in general)

Buying a canoe is not always as simple as looking for an inexpensive new or used aluminum sixteen foot square back. You may need to give more thought to the design before you drop several hundred bucks (minimum). Will it be used in open water, or on small ponds where portage may be a problem? Do you want aluminum, plastic, wood, or composites?

Wood canoes are laborious for the industry to build and are somewhat fragile, but they do have the advantage of allowing good hull shapes. In fact, topnotch designers often make experimental canoe designs from wood to test new ideas. Wood is well suited to building single prototypes and allows much design freedom.

Aluminum on the other hand, allows little freedom. The material has limits, as does the manufacturing process. The curves needed for the sleek-yet-stable hull are hard to form from aluminum. Also the bow and stern can't be slim since room must be left to rivet the hull sides together.

Finally, since expensive dies are needed for aluminum, both sides are stamped from one die. Thus the bow and stern are identical, and the widest point is midway along the hull. Ideally, the bow and stern should be shaped specifically for their functions, and the widest point should be aft (back) of center to give a sleeker bow.

The plastic used for canoes are polyethylene and Royalex. Some builders rename these materials, but you will definitely know a canoe is plastic if it's claim to fame is near indestructibility. The fact is however, these hulls can be damaged, but they are durable indeed. Rarely is good design or performance claimed for plastic hulls, but that may not be a strong suite for waterfowlers anyway. This claim is more for the purest, or the racer.

If designed with performance in mind, which is rare, hull flexing causes plastic canoes to be less than satisfactory. To perform well, a canoe must be rigid to hold its proper shape and be just flexible enough to absorb impact. Plastics (especially polyethylene) are very flexible but not rigid. Due to excessive flexing, even a well shaped plastic canoe does not paddle as well as it should.

Although plastic allows better designs than aluminum, few plastic canoes are well designed, and even they rank far below the performance offered by the composites.

Composite canoes are made by bonding fibers together with resins inside a mold. The best-known fiber is the one we are all familiar with, namely fiberglass. But the name is so vague as to convey little information. There are many, varied fabrics that are actually fiberglass, but the term is also erroneously used to include Kevlar, graphite, Tuf-weave, or other composite fibers that are not fiberglass. The appeal of composite canoes is that they can be designed for excellent performance, but also have very good durability.

The fact that composite canoes can be designed for superb paddling however, doesn't mean all are. To get a well-designed canoe, you should be aware of hull design and know who the performance builders are. Canoe publications or clubs can help in this regard. Armed with the facts, you are able to find a canoe that is ideal for you whether waterfowling or simply paddling down a stream on a spring day looking for a few tasty Brookies.

Any comparison of canoes must include dimensions and shape. Shape is more important but harder to explain. So let's look at dimension first.

Length is crucial. A six-inch increase in length makes a notable improvement in tracking, speed, and gliding ability, and will carry more weight with less loss of performance. These are the basic laws of physics.

Short canoes turn sharper, tend to be lighter, and cost less. But weight and price are governed more by construction than actual size. Thus, the only **absolute** virtue of the short canoe is quicker turning. For waterfowlers, a minimum 14-15 foot canoe is almost a must if you expect to carry any reasonable load, including another hunter and a retriever.

Width is important too. Its major effect is upon stability. But it's a misconception that a wide hull guarantees stability.

Stability has been sometimes defined as *initial* and *final*, or *primary* and *secondary*; or whenever your overweight lab tips you over in a November blow. The terms don't matter, especially in the later example, but the idea does matter. Initial stability is steadiness when upright. Final stability is ultimate resistance to a capsize. For now however, accept that *shape* more than width governs stability. A narrow hull design can be stable, but can't have lots of both types. Thus good designers plan narrow hulls seeking more final stability.

Wide hulls can have both types of stability if designed well, but few probably are. Wide hulls get initial stability from width, yet most are shaped to give even more of it. Therefore, most wide hulls have far too much stability yet little final stability. A wide hull feels safe upright, but that's certainly no promise it resists overturning.

More width also adds capacity, but not as much as length would. A long hull actually holds more and performs better loaded.

The final crucial point is that width harms efficiency. A wide hull pushes more water which requires more effort. Period.

Depth is the last major dimension. To increase it adds freeboard, capacity and seaworthiness and it doesn't affect tracking, speed or turning. Thus it may seem that extra depth is always a bonus. But too much depth isn't always a bonus if it causes wind resistance. Try setting out decoys or picking them up on a windy day and you will quickly learn this lesson.

Any wind from the sides or quarters causes steering problems that extra freeboard exaggerates. Excess freeboard also makes it hard to paddle comfortably. With the heavy gear that waterfowlers tend to pack along, and rough waters we sometimes encounter, the extra freeboard is valuable for sure.

Canoes, regardless of their size, float and move just as yachts, barges and battleships do. To float, a canoe displaces water equal in weight to the hull and load. If your canoe weighs 125 pounds for example, and you weigh 170 pounds, your retriever at 80 pounds (dry), and the rest of your gear is 70 pounds, the displacement must be (125 + 170 + 80 + 70) 445 pounds equivlent to the weight of water. A gallon of water weighs 8.33 pounds and a cubic foot weighs slightly over 62 pounds. Divide 62 into 445 pounds and you discover that you need to displace slightly over seven cubic feet of water to float the above weighted canoe. Add a waterlogged Golden Retriever, and you end up with another cubic foot of replacement. This may be a bit on the techy side, but it's interesting.

Canoes don't skim the water, they pass through it, pushing it aside, then allowing it to return. In the process the hull interacts with the water in ways that influence speed, glide, capacity, stability, and maneuverability.

A few words about "rocker" should be noted at this point. Viewed from the side, the bottom of a canoe hull may be level, may curve up at the ends, or may curve entirely from bow to stern. This curve is called rocker, and plays a major role with turning. With lots of rocker, a hull turns easily; in fact, it doesn't want to go straight. The bow and stern draw little water to present less hinderance to turn and give less help to track. Rocker makes a hull act shorter than it is, adding maneuverability, but harming streamlining. For waterfowlers, straight line is more important, unless you plan on running a slalom through your decoys.

As to keels, it's widely thought a keel is used for tracking (keeping in a straight line). Actually, most hulls with a keel (aluminum hulls especially) need it for strength with no function related to performance. A keel helps a poor design track, but a good design needs no keel. Enough said.

The least understood part of canoe, and consequently the most important to stability and safety is called *cross-section shape.* Some hulls feel steady when upright, and many people take this as proof of high resistance to capsizing. Like David Copperfield's seemingly magic performances, it is actually only an illusion.

Remember that earlier it was stated that initial stability is a hull's steadiness when upright or nearly so, and final stability is ultimate resistance to capsizing as the hull nears capsize. Which then, is more important?

There's no value in false security, i.e., lots of initial stability. There's real value in resistance to capsizing, i.e., lots of final stability. So if a hull favors one form as often as it must, final stability is the sensible choice.

Flat-bottom hulls have little final stability. Johnboats are good examples. They feel steady when level, but tip suddenly on waves or if leaned to a critical angle. The opposite of flat bottom (a perfectly round one), would act the opposite way, feeling the same at any angle of lean. Unfortunately, it would always be at the same lean, and would have no initial stability. This is why no canoes are perfectly rounded.

Now comes compromise. Shallow arch canoes give up some initial stability to gain more final stability and predictability. But to complicate matters, arched hulls don't all behave alike, since one may be nearly flat, another nearly round, and all stages in between.

The last type of hull is the shallow Vee. It's like an arch but with a ridge (like a keel) in the center. Compared to a hull of similar shape, the stability of a Vee is much the same, but the ridge has a negative effect on what is called the surface-to-volume ratio, so it increases water resistance. Not a problem with waterfowlers, unless you race.

These are all of the hull aspects below the waterline. Shape above the water is important as well. By planning shape above the water, designers impart extra safety that comes into play only when needed.

One idea is to flare the hull out near the top to deflect waves and give extra resistance to capsize. Flare is useful on canoes for rapids or wind-driven waves.

If you are still with me in this article, you will now have more information on canoe (or small boat) technology than most of your friends. How you use it and what value it has to you is entirely your call. If you are in the market for a new canoe, than I suspect this information will assist you in that choice.

(Note: I wish to thank Dave Kruger of We-No-Nah Canoe Co., We-No-Nah, MN for the technical portions of this article. His assistance and permission to use this information is appreciated).

LENGTH

Longer canoes will have greater hull speed, will track better, and will have greater potential for carrying capacity. Shorter canoes will be more maneuverable and lighter in weight.

WIDTH

Widths, or beams as they are called, are given in two measurements; the beam at the gunwale and the beam at the 4" waterline. The 4" waterline beam has the greatest influence on performance. Wide beamed canoes offer great stability but may be somewhat slow. Narrow canoes may be less stable but afford better efficiency and hull speed.

DEPTH

Greater depth allows for increased carrying capacity and better water shedding ability. However, deep canoes can be harder to handle in windy conditions and will be heavier.

The shape of the bottom of the canoe and how it blends with the sides will influence its performance. Stability of a canoe is affected greatly by its cross section.

ENTRY LINES

The shape of the bow where it cuts the water will have an effect on the canoe's performance. A very sharp, knife-like entry will cut through the water easily and provide efficiency. A blunt bow will add fullness and give buoyancy in waves, thus a drier ride.

SYMMETRY

Symmetrical canoes have identical ends, bow and stern. Symmetrical canoes offer more versatile designs and convert more readily from tandem to solo.

Asymmetrical canoes are usually designed for a particular specialty.

CROSS SECTION

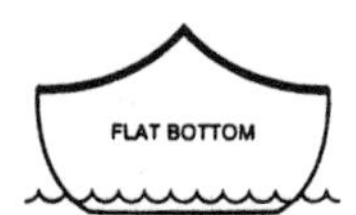

Flat bottom

Flat bottom canoes offer great initial stability. That is, they feel very secure on calm water. Flat bottom canoes are great for the sportsmen and general recreationalists looking for steadiness.

Shallow arch bottom

Shallow arch bottom canoes have less initial stability but good secondary stability. As the canoe is leaned, it will balance on its side and resist further tipping Shallow arch canoes work well in waves and whitewater. Shallow arch bottom canoes offer the best all-around performance.

Round bottom

Round bottom canoes have great secondary stability but very little initial stability. The are designed for speed and efficiency. Round bottom canoes are usually fast, specialized canoes.

Keels

A keel will help tracking in short canoes and will help the canoe's resistance to crosswinds. Keels also work well on canoes used with outboard or electric motors, as they decrease sideslipping.

A keel would not be preferred on a canoe used in whitewater or situations where quick maneuvers are essential.

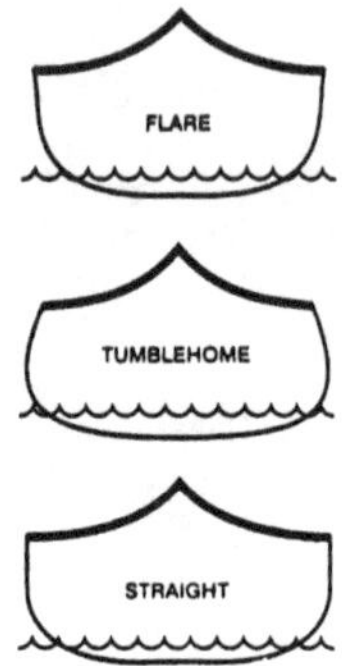

Flare, Tumblehome, Straight-sided

The sides of the canoe can have flare, tumblehome or be straight-sided. Flare will shed water well and increase stability. Tumblehome gives a narrower beam at the gunwales and allows for easier paddling, however stability will be decreased. Straight-sided canoes are a compromise of the two.

Keep in mind that many canoes will incorporate one, two, or all three of these in different areas of the hull.

Canoes are great for getting to those areas that are generally inaccessible to larger watercraft, especially shallow water sites such as this flooded corn field.

Commercial

Boats, Blinds & Related Gear

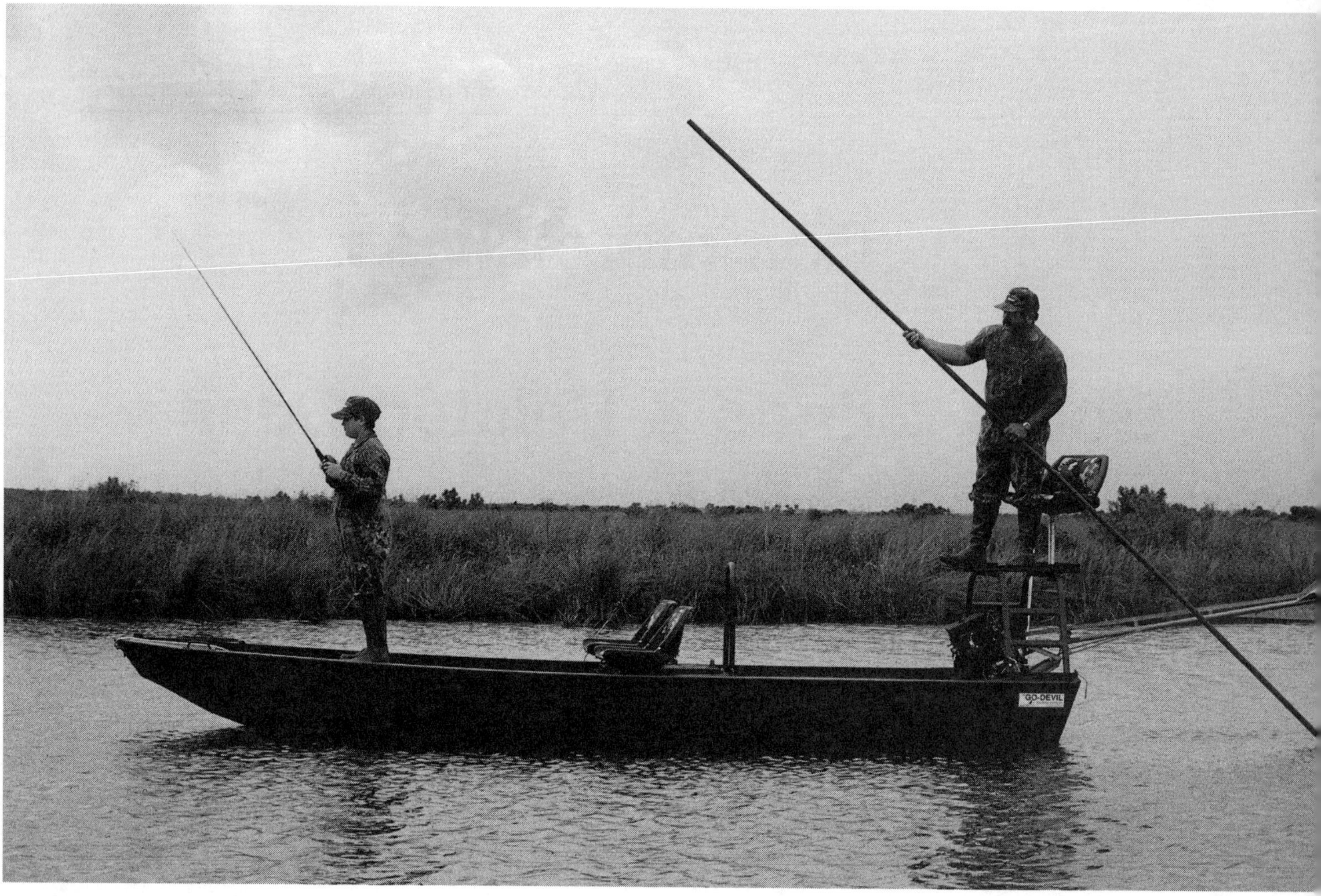

The Go-Devil® Duck Hunting & Fishing Boa

Designed for the Go-Devil ® to go where other boats can't!

.100 or .125 aluminum hull. No wood in transom!

Slick bottom and round chines. No crimps or keels.

Large dry storage under seat. Flotation to meet Coast Guard standards!

GO-DEVIL®

Go-Devil® Engines available for your boat in 5.5, 9, 16, 20 & 25 HP

For more information call
(504) 752-0167
Go-Devil® Mfg. of Louisiana, Inc.
18469 Womack Rd.
Baton Rouge, LA 70817

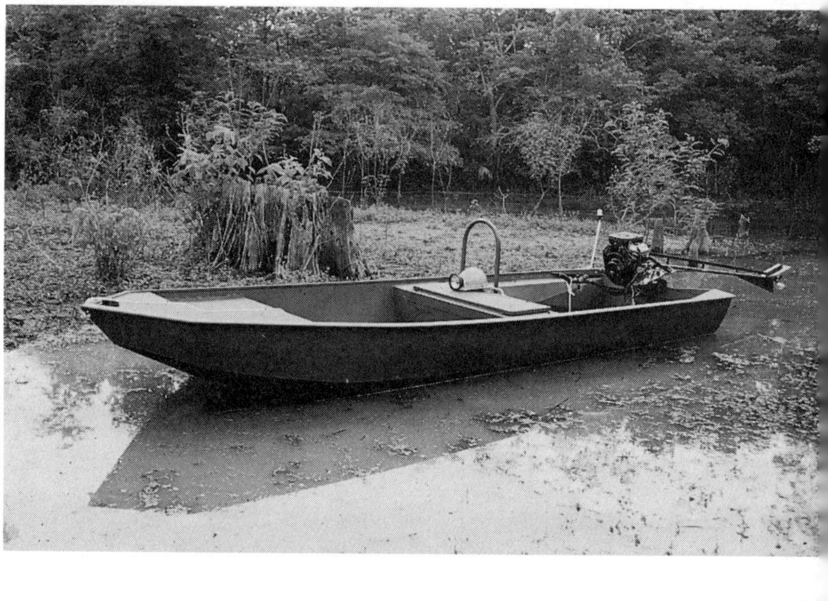

▲ Quick Pro Blind accommodates one to three hunters (five with Extension Kit)

The Only Versatile Blind For ALL Your Waterfowl Hunting

Versatile and Durable

Permanent, but readily portable - ideal for field, marsh, shore or boat

Accommodates one to three hunters and dog -four to five hunters with Extension Kit

Ten minutes to assemble or disassemble without tools - frame interlocks securely

Flip-Top provides 100% concealment - drops down instantly for quick shooting

Netting permits 360° viewing - so tough, it can be left up all season!

Entire blind and Flip-Top being transported in the custom carrybag/backpack ▼

Specifications

High impact, lightweight PVC frame, camo colored throughout

Frame is waterproof, fade resistant - won't crack, chip or splinter!

Genuine military camouflage - reversible netting is made of polypropylene with 3-D rubberized vinyl leaf; resists fading, rot, tearing, fire and remains flexible in all temperatures

Netting allows easy brushing with natural vegetation

Camouflage options to match corn, field, timber, reed, bulrush or marsh

Quick Pro® Blind camo fastening system allows rapid camo set-up

Blind and Flip-Top conveniently fit in custom carrybag/backpack

▲ Flip-Top conceals completely; drops instantly for quick shooting

To order, or for FREE brochure, call Toll-Free:

1-888- TJ BLIND (1-888-852-5463)

T &J, L.L.C. • The Quick Pro® Blind Company • PO Box 386 • Martinsville, NJ 08836

Hunt Smart.
BE INVISIBLE.
Endorsed by Hunters, Professional Guides & Hunting Clubs.
• No Assembly
• Very Low Profile
• Spring Loaded Lid
• Built-in Floor
• Reclined Seating
• Fully Collapsible
• Aluminum Frame
• Cordura Covers
• Only 12 pounds
• Built to Last
"Concealment is no longer a concern."
THE ELIMINATOR™
BY FINAL APPROACH™
Call to order Unbelievable Up-Close Action Videos!
P.O. Box 146
Murphy, Oregon 97533
(541) 476-7562
VISA
MasterCard
FINAL APPROACH™

Portable Pit Blind The "UNIPIT" gives you TOTAL CONCEALMENT – even on naked soil, and it's HIGHLY PORTABLE and EASY TO INSTALL.

You will thoroughly enjoy hunting from its comfortable, reclined position. The "UNIPIT" is also completely weatherproof and warm. Tested in sub-zero weather, the durable Poly Plastic material will not break. The solid one piece lower unit is waterproof and can be placed in up to 12 inches of water and mud without leaking. The easy flip lid, has even been designed with a waterproof hinge area to withstand heavy rain. The pit blind weighs an approx. 33 pounds and can be stacked one inside another, for easy transportation and storage. Filled with decoys, you can drag it anywhere, it even floats, while crossing water.

Removing 4 to 10 inches of soil, the low profile design enables installation to be completed in 15-25 minutes. This pit blind can be installed anywhere and the more out in the open, the better. STOP WORRYING about what camouflage pattern to use. Simply cover the lower half of the blind with soil and attach the surrounding fodder to the flip lid. It's always PERFECT!

From the air, even the weariest of waterfowl will reveal only your decoys and wide open soil. NO SUSPICIOUS LUMPS OR BRUSH PILES TO FLY WIDE OF. You will not experience closer landings from any other blind system.

When finished, take your "UNIPIT" home or simply attach the overnight lid and leave it in place for weeks to come. Our photos give examples where we hunt with the "UNIPIT" and see for yourself, total concealment that's tough on waterfowl. The "UNIPIT" holds one individual, up to approximately 6'3", 240 lbs.

Your portable pit blind will include: detailed instructions to improve your hunting success, (1ea.) insulated mat, 27 feet of camo cord, (1ea.) overnight lid, (1ea.) 4 ft. tow rope, assorted hardware and a 1-year warranty against material and manufacturer defects. Some assembly is required.

The suggested retail price of $259.99 is much less than surface type blinds and saves you much more money, not needing all of those camouflage patterns. Start getting the most for your money today and those large harvests that you've always dreamed of, in the comfort of a "UNIPIT" Portable Pit Blind.

For our full color brochure, contact:

North Central Outfitters

R.D.2 Box 682 • Lock Haven, PA 17745

Toll Free 1- 888-88-BLIND • 717-748-6699 • FAX 717-748-5915 attn: Patrick Ward

The Muskrat Skiff
The Long Point Skiff
The Chesapeake
The Hercules Lay-Out
One Man Lay-Out Boat

THE BOAT BLIND™

End Your Hunt for the Perfect Blind

No method of waterfowl hunting gives you the versatility, mobility and effectiveness of a boat blind — and no boat blind is built better than a blind by Canvas Works. The Boat Blind™ has all the features serious waterfowlers look for in a blind: perfect concealment, durability, lightweight and a customized fit.

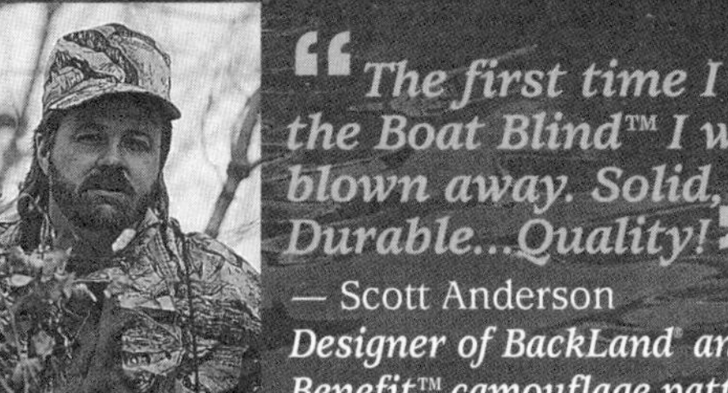

"The first time I saw the Boat Blind™ I was blown away. Solid, Durable...Quality!"

— Scott Anderson
Designer of BackLand® and Full Benefit™ camouflage patterns. Professional hunter

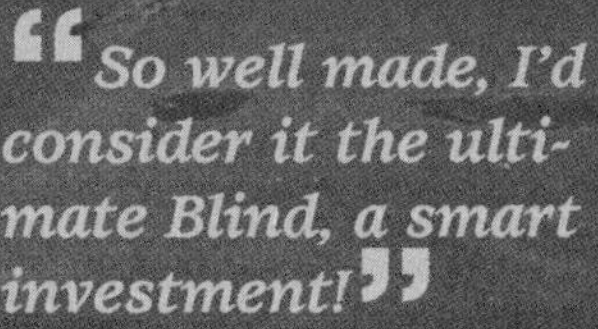

"So well made, I'd consider it the ultimate Blind, a smart investment!"

— Randy Bartz
Professional guide, originator of the T-Flag Known as the FlagMan™ BackLand® PRO STAFF MEMBER

"Practical, very effective, will last a lifetime, a must have!"

— Gary McCree
World renowned guide, championship caller Manufacturer of Goose Master Calls™ BackLand® PRO STAFF MEMBER

Constructed for a lifetime of waterfowl hunting. Heavy duty, poly-coated 1000 Denier Cordura® nylon keeps you dry and comfortable during ideal hunting conditions — rain, snow and wind. Double strength aluminum tubing and virtually unbreakable Vislon® fittings stand up to the most demanding hunters and conditions. Giant #10 YKK® zippers eliminate the possibility of frozen zippers and enable you to open shooting windows with gloves.

The Boat Blind's™ rugged construction allows you to leave the blind set up at all times — even when traveling down the highway. Canvas Works can customize your fishing boat or old hunting boat into a serious waterfowling machine. Every blind is built to your specifications and backed by a two year warranty.

Options that will increase your success and comfort. Custom built gun cases, dog platforms and ladders add convenience to your hunt. Vegetation loops and holders and a motor cover ensure total concealment. A unique boat side cover completely hides your boat and puts your blind right to the water. All Canvas Works custom boat blinds and blind accessories are available in extremely versatile and effective BackLand® All-Terrain™ camo the choice of serious waterfowlers.

Turn your boat into a custom blind.

Duane Smith's Custom Canvas Works
4144 Shoreline Drive P.O. Box 44
Spring Park, MN 55384

Phone (612) 471-7763 Fax (612) 471-7794

R.I.P. Blind
(Ready In Position)

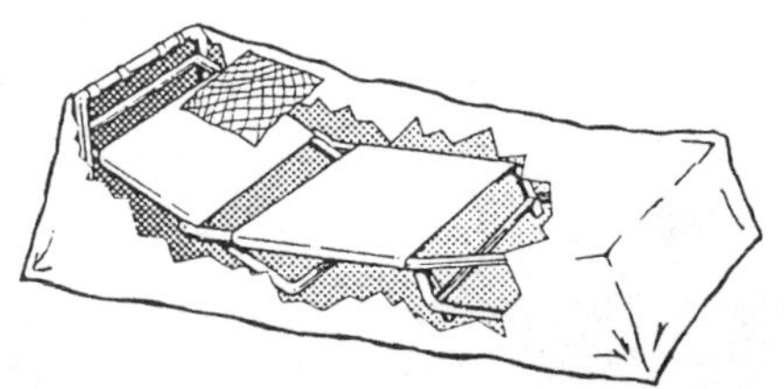

The **R.I.P. Blind** eliminates laying in a muddy field or spending time digging pits. Set-up time is literally in seconds. A self-contained low profile lay-down blind with a chair built into the frame-work, which is made of one inch tubular steel, with a spring-loaded cover made of 500 Denier Cordura. The hunter is completely covered until it is time to shoot, then you simply push the release button allowing the lid to fly open giving you a 360° shooting radius. The Blind weighs 24 pounds with dimensions of 10 x 42 x 32 inches when folded or 92 x 32 x 26 inches when laid ready to use.

The Original
Sittin' Goose Decoy Blind

The **Sittin' Goose Decoy Blind** is today's revolution in blinds. This blind will eliminate laying in a muddy field, or spending time digging pits, enabling the hunter to concentrate on the day's activity. Weighing in at 14 pounds, this Sittin' Goose Decoy Blind is a portable unit which folds up to a handy 45 x 23 inch pack for easy one-man carrying. Set-up is made simple by embedding the spiked back legs into the ground for quick hunting. This Blind has a water-resistant camouflage 500 denier cordura seat covering to add comfort to your hunting. The goose decoy is affixed to the chair to enable the hunter to camouflage himself yet flip it back to score his prey. The goose decoy head is randomly selected with the option of feeder or sentry head. Assembly is requires. Made in the U.S.A.

Woods Calls Inc.• PO Box 29434 • Lincoln, NE 68529

CALL 1-800-336-5197 for a FREE catalog which includes both of these blinds as well as other products manufactured by Woods Calls.

TRAX AMERICA, INC.

Tag-A-Long

Carry two of your hunting buddies and all their gear in armchair comfort. Great for dropping off deer hunters at their tree stands, bird hunters in the fields, and duck hunters at their stands.

Duck Buggy

The Duck Buggy is easily transportable with its 6 x 8 foot floats, fitting easily inside a light-duty trailer. Its blind size is 4 x 6 feet, with a load capacity of 1,000 pounds. Features include Advantage camo, QuickShoot flop-top, rain top, and hinged entry door.

Boat Blind

An infinite number of adjustments allow you to position both sides of your boat to accommodate different situations. No tools necessary for assembly. Folds neatly inside of boat for transporting.

Check out our Boat Motor Cover, Dog Stand, Tree Stands, and other quality outdoor items.

FOR CATALOG OF PRODUCTS CALL OR WRITE:

TRAX AMERICA, INC.
BOX 898, FORREST CITY, AR 72336-0898
1-800-232-2327 Fax (501)633-4788

CATTAIL CAMO®

160 and 330 Denier Cordura nylon for duck blinds

- 60-inch-wide fabric
- 5-yard minimum
- Brush Camo® and Konifer® available

CATTAIL CAMO® GEAR BAGS

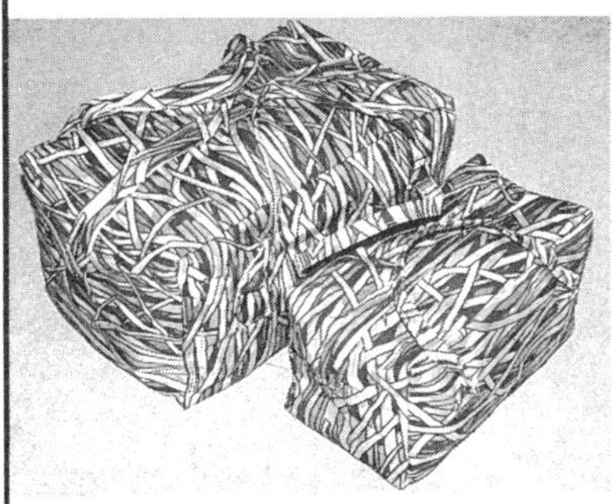

Quality starts with 1000 Denier Cordura nylon, the toughest fabric available for gear bags. Water-repellent polyurethane finish.

Save $10
Tote—~~*$59.95*~~ ***$49.95***
(9 × 10 × 17 in.)

Save $15
Gear—~~*$74.95*~~ ***$59.95***
(13 × 12 × 23 in.)

LARRY SANBURG FABRICS

932 Main Street
Manson, Iowa 50563
712/469-3628

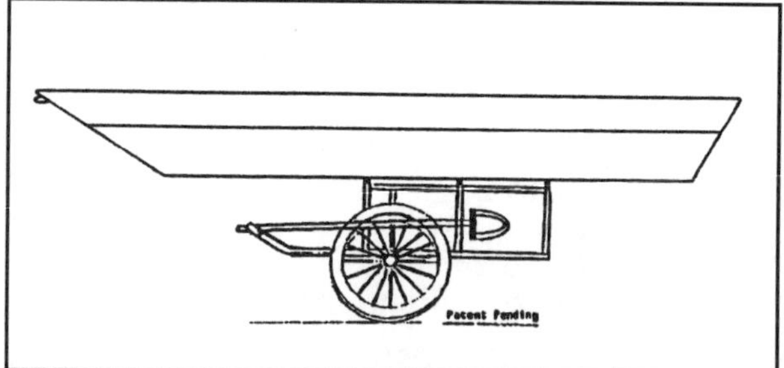

*GAME CARRIER ***DECOY HAULER**
*BOAT HAULER *FIREWOOD HAULER
*EQUIPMENT CARRIER
***BOAT TRANSPORTER**

"The serious cart with the funny angled wheels"

For More Information Contact:

NXT SHOT VERSACART TM
950 CLEARWATER RD
NORTH AUGUSTA, GA 29841

(803)593-9282

BOATS & BLOCKS by BUSICK

1 & 2 MAN FIBERGLASS LAKE ERIE LAYOUTS

CUSTOM BUILT WATERFOWLING CRAFT

-- also available --

Plans & Full Size Patterns for Lake Erie Layouts

Lake Erie Layout Rib Kits

Award Winning Gunning Decoys

Decorative Waterfowl Carvings

Waterfowling Accessories

Paul A. Busick

174 Edgewood Drive, Dept. B Amherst, Ohio 44001

Phone (216) 988-7160

Folding PORTA-BOTE
8'-10'-12' Lengths

Call or write for FREE BROCHURE

Porta-Bote International
1074 Independence Ave.
Mountain View, CA 94043

(800)227-8882 * FAX (650)961-3800

Internet: www.porta-bote.com
-mail address: info@porta-bote.com

WATERFOWLING BOATS, BLINDS AND RELATED GEAR BOOK PURCHASE

Issues of this book can be purchased from certain sporting outlets, catalogs, magazines, sportsman groups, or direct from the address listed below. Please copy and complete the following order blank. Books normally are mailed within 4-5 days of receipt of order.

Name______________________________
(Please Print)

Address______________________________ City____________________

State________ Zip______________

Number of books________@ $17.95 each. Subtotal______________

S/H______________

Sales Tax (If applicable)______________

Total______________

Please add **$3.00 S/H** for the first book, $2.00 for each additional book.
Michigan residents add 6% sales tax ($1.08 per book). Please send check or money orders to:

Outdoor Publications
POB 6670
Saginaw, MI 48608

NOTES

NOTES

NOTES

Boat Terminology

Aft: facing toward the stern or back of the boat.
Angle Iron: usually flat, "L-shaped" lengths of iron as opposed to "tubular" iron or steel.
Beam: the greatest width of a boat.
Bilge: the lower interior areas of a hull.
Bilge Pump: a mechanical pump used to remove standing water in the bottom (bilge area) of a boat.
Bow: front end of a boat.
Bulkhead: the vertical partitions, corresponding to the walls in house.
Camber: to arch a deck allowing water to drain off.
Chine: a well-defined angle of a boat where the bottom meets the sides.
Cleats: metal or wood fittings that are used to tie-off or attach a line.
Combings: the vertical pieces around the edges of cockpits, hatches, etc.
Cockpit: open areas of a boat,(e.g. where hunters sit/stand.)
Coffin Blind: generally considered a field or shallow water blind (measured in inches rather than feet) where hunter is "layed out" in a box made of fiberglass providing a low profile effect.
Composite Construction: the use of two or more materials (e.g.two types of wood or a wood/ metal combo) in the construction of the hull of a boat.
Conduit: tubular metal or plastic components used for the support frame of a blind.
Cure: the time it takes for a resin to harden, usually time/temperature dependent: i.e. high temperature, shorter cure time; low temperature, longer cure time.
Danforth Anchor: a common type of anchor used to bury-in to the ground with high holding power.
Draft: the depth of water required to float a boat.
Dry Rot: the rotting of wood on a boat as a result of the invasion of a fungus.
Even Keel: the term used when a boat floats properly in the water.
Fairing: filling in areas on a boat (building up the surface) to make them blend more evenly with the surrounding surface.
Glass: short name for fiberglass.
Glassing: a term used for fiberglassing a wood boat with a resin.
GPS: Global Positioning System; used as an electronic directional source, making use of satellites.
Grommets: a ring made of metal or plastic used to fasten a rope; a metal or plastic eyelet.
Gunning Platform: the area on a platform blind where hunters sit or stand while getting ready to shoot.
Gunwales: (pronounced gun'l; sometimes incorrectly spelled gunnel or gunwhale); the top plank around the outer edge of a boat.
Hatch: openings in deck to provide access below.
Heel: a boat that is leaning off its vertical.
Hull: the basic part of a boat without any equipment (e.g. seats).
Jet Drive: an outboard that uses water thrust (jets) rather than a propeller for movement.
Johnboat: usually considered a flat bottom boat with a square bow (sometimes incorrectly spelled "jon")
Keel: the major longitudinal member of a boat hull (bottom/center).
Laminating: bonding together two or more layers of wood strips, planks, veneers or sheets of wood.
Layout: refers to a layout boat.
Layout Boat: a boat specifically constructed to give a hunter a low profile in open water; generally used for diver ducks, but also effective for puddlers.
Lists: the term used when a boat inclines (leans) to port or starboard.
Motor Mount: the area on the stern of a boat where the motor attaches.
Pit Blind: a blind that is dug out in a field; may be several inches or feet, depending on the conditions.
Pop Rivet:a metal fastener used for joining various parts of a boat.
Port: left side of boat when facing forward (the word "left" has four letters and so does "port").
Pram: similar to a johnboat; flatbottom, square stern, but generally smaller in overall size.

Prop: the blade portion of the lower unit of a boat motor that drives the boat.
Pumpkinseed: a term that is sometimes used to describe or refer to a layout boat.
Punt Pole: a long pole used to push a boat through shallow water areas, especially where motors have a problem with weeds or water depth.
PVC: Poly Vinyl Chloride; referred to in this book as a plastic tubing used for framing a blind.
Ribbing: cross support pieces running perpendicular to the vertical on the floor of a boat.
Rig: a slang term used to describe a boat, including the blind.
Rub Rail: a piece of rail that extends away from a boat to help protect the boat from rubbing on docks, etc.
Sculling: a method of sneaking up on resting ducks in a specialized boat, aptly called a sculling boat.
Sink Box: a box that is designed to be almost completely submerged below the waterline for hiding a hunter.
Sneak Boat: a boat designed, as the name implies, for sneaking up on resting waterfowl, often referred to as a sculling boat.
Square Stern: refers to a flat rather than a pointed (like the front of a canoe) backside (stern) of a boat where the motor is mounted.
Starboard: right side of a boat when facing forward.
Stem: the leading edge of a hull; the major structural section of the bow on a wooden boat.
Stern: back of a boat.
Swamps: the term used when a boat fills with water.
Swamp Seat: a piece of wood or other material cut approximately 3-4 feet long with a short cross piece attached to the top, that is stuck in the mud or water and used by a waterfowl hunter for resting or leaning on while hunting.
Templates: a precut design (pattern) out of paper, cardboard, plywood or other suitable material, used to reproduce an original of something.
Transom: the flat area across the stern (where motor is mounted).
Trim: the way in which a boat floats in the water.
Waterline: the plane where the surface of the water touches the hull when normally loaded.
Winch: a mechanical piece of equipment used as a crank for pulling.

WATERFOWLER'S CHECK LIST

General Items:
( )Flashlight (waterproof/floating)
( )Spotlight
( )Knife
( )Machete
( )Decoys
( )Motor
( )Gas tank
( )License(s)
( )Outboard oil mix
( )Motor repair kit/tools
( )Extra prop/shear pins
( )Insect spray
( )Emergency gear (e.g. Flares)
( )Cooler
( )Paddles
( )Anchor
( )Drain plug
( )Calls
( )Gun
( )Gun cleaning kit
( )Shells
( )Shell box
( )Life preserver(s)
( )Floating Gun Case
( )Wader repair kit
( )Food/drink
( )Camo covering(s)
( )Binoculars
( )Sunglasses
( )Reading/Eye glasses
( )Rope
( )Seats
( )First aid kit
( )Compass
( )Copy of waterfowl regulations
( )Duck ID book
( )Punt pole
( )Layout boat decoy lines
( )Weights for decoy lines
( )Heater(s)
( )Hand Cream/Lip Balm
( )
( )
( )
( )
( )

Retriever Items:
( )Lead
( )Collar
( )Whistle
( )Training dummy
( )First Aid kit
( )Medicine
( )Dog ladder
( )Neoprene jacket
( )Food/Energy Snacks
( )
( )

Clothing:
( )Rain gear
( )Gloves
( )(Extra) warm clothing/gloves
( )Waterproof bag for storage of extra clothing
( )Hat
( )Waders
( )Boots
( )Camo coat
( )Camo pants
( )Face covering
( )Insulated underclothes
( )
( )
( )
( )

Electronics:
( )Two-way radios
( )Marine radio
( )Weather radio
( )GPS
( )Radio
( )Extra Batteries
( )Battery Charger(s)
( )Camera
( )Cellular Phone
( )
( )